No Other Success

No Other Success

THE PARENTING PRACTICES OF
DAVID O. MCKAY

MARK D. OGLETREE

Published by the Religious Studies Center, Brigham Young University, Provo, Utah, in cooperation with Deseret Book Company, Salt Lake City.

Visit us at rsc.byu.edu.

Printed in the United States of America by Sheridan Books, Inc.

DESERET BOOK is a registered trademark of Deseret Book Company.

Visit us at DeseretBook.com.

Cover and interior design by Madison Swapp.

ISBN: 978-1-9443-9414-1
Price: $17.99

Library of Congress Cataloging-in-Publication Data

Names: Ogletree, Mark D., 1962- author.
Title: No other success : the parenting practices of David O. McKay / Mark D. Ogletree.
Description: Provo : Religious Studies Center BYU, [2017] | Includes index.
Identifiers: LCCN 2016051262 | ISBN 9781944394141 (alk. paper)
Subjects: LCSH: McKay, David O. (David Oman), 1873-1970. | Fatherhood--Religious aspects--Church of Jesus Christ of Latter-day Saints. | Parenting--Religious aspects--Church of Jesus Christ of Latter-day Saints.
Classification: LCC BX8643.F3 O34 2017 | DDC 248.8/421--dc23 LC record available at https://lccn.loc.gov/2016051262

Contents

Ancestors and Descendants of David O. McKay

Margaret Powell	Thomas Evans
b. 7/2/1813	b. 10/?/1812
d. 10/9/1896	d. 5/25/1877

Jennette Eveline Evans
b. 8/28/1850
d. 1/5/1905

Margaret Elizabeth McKay	Elena Odette McKay	David Oman McKay	Thomas Evans McKay	Jeanette Isabel McKay
b. 1/22/1869	b. 5/22/1871	b. 9/8/1873	b. 10/29/1875	b. 11/12/1879
d. 3/28/1880	d. 4/1/1880	d. 1/18/1970	d. 1/15/1958	d. 3/30/1971

Emma Ray Riggs
b. 6/23/1877
m. 1/2/1901
d. 11/14/1970

David Lawrence McKay	Llewelyn Riggs McKay	Louise Jeanette McKay	Royle Riggs McKay
b. 9/30/1901	b. 6/5/1904	b. 10/13/1906	b. 10/21/1909
d. 10/27/1993	d. 1/2/1975	d. 12/16/2002	d. 4/9/1912

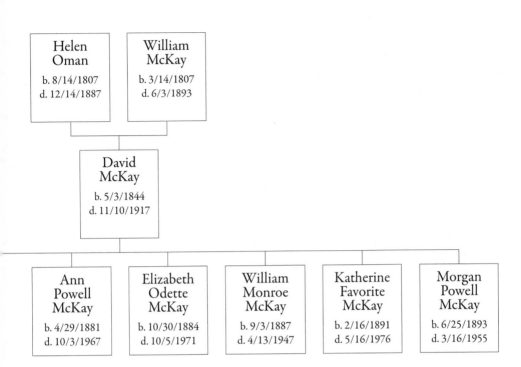

A Fathering Crisis

"No other success can compensate for failure in the home."[1]
—J. E. McCullough

There is a fathering crisis in our nation, and American families must wake up and face reality. The fatherhood debacle that emerged in the 1990s has not disappeared as many have supposed. If anything, the problem has continued to gain momentum. In a 2006 survey, 91 percent of the respondents *strongly* or *somewhat agree* that there is a crisis of father absence in our country.[2] In May of 2011, in a front-page story featured in the *Deseret News* entitled "Fatherless America?," Elizabeth Stuart reported that one-third of American children are growing up without their biological father in the home. According to the US Census Bureau, during the past fifty years, the percentage of children who live with two married parents has dropped twenty-two points. Meanwhile, the number of babies born to unwed mothers has jumped from 5 percent to 40 percent.[3]

Father absence is such a pressing social issue that every United States President since Bill Clinton has addressed the consequences of a fatherless society. Former President George W. Bush declared:

> Over the past four decades, fatherlessness has emerged as one of our greatest social problems. We know that children who grow up with absent fathers can suffer lasting damage. They are more likely to end up in poverty or drop out of school, become addicted to drugs, have a child out of wedlock or end up in prison. Fatherlessness is not the only cause of these things, but our nation must recognize it as an important factor.[4]

According to a Gallup poll, seven in ten adults believe that a child needs both a mother and a father in the home to be happy.[5] However, there is often a significant gap between the ideal and the real. For example, in America, 24.35 million children (33.5 percent) live absent of their biological father,[6] and of students in grades 1–12, 39 percent live in fatherless homes.[7]

Father Irrelevance

Nonetheless, every child in America is *not* without a father. The good news is that most men in America live with their children; therefore, father absence is not a problem that the majority of American families contend with. Perhaps a more universal problem is father irrelevance. Too many fathers in our society are not necessarily absent from their homes, but they are certainly uninvolved in the lives of their children. These men are often disconnected emotionally, socially, and certainly spiritually.[8] Perhaps much of this trend is driven by the economic conditions of contemporary families. Fathers seem to be working longer hours to supply their children with material possessions and to pay down their own debts. Harvard psychiatrist Dr. Robert Coles further explained:

> Parents are too busy spending their most precious capital—their time and their energy—struggling to keep up with *MasterCard* payments. . . . They work long hours to barely keep up, and when they get home at the end of the day they're tired. And their kids are left with a Nintendo or a pair of Nikes or some other piece of [junk]. Big deal.[9]

In a Gallup opinion poll, 96 percent of the respondents said that their families were either extremely important or very important.[10] Once again, most of us seem to understand what matters most in life. There is a disconnect between how we live and the way we believe. Even though many American fathers value their family and make sacrifices for their children, it appears that too many are unwilling to spend time with their children on a regular basis. Unfortunately, many American fathers are spinning their wheels as they seek to bless their children with material possessions. First of all, most children do not express gratitude for their father's hard work or for what he is providing. Second, deep down, most children would rather have time with their dad than a new trinket of some sort.

Moreover, the time famine causes fathers to feel guilty for not being home as much as they should. By the time a father answers to a boss, work demands, or the bill collector, there is very little time left for his children. Too many fathers today feel that purchasing material goods for their children is the primary method of showing love.[11] For them, materialism compensates for involvement.

The Time Famine

Today, 70 percent of fathers and mothers feel that they do not have enough time to spend with their children.[12] Consider that a child in a two-parent family will spend, on average, 1.2 hours each weekday and 3.3 hours on a weekend day directly interacting with his or her father. Overall, the average total time fathers are accessible to their children is 2.5 hours on weekdays and 6.3 hours on weekend days.[13] Economist Juliet Schor has argued that over the past two decades the average worker had added 164 hours—a month of work—to their work year.[14]

Despite all of this, most fathers would like to be home more often and spend more time with their children. A MasterCard survey found that almost 85 percent of fathers claimed that "the most priceless gift of all" was time spent with family.[15] Furthermore, 62 percent of fathers reported that they would be willing to sacrifice job opportunities and higher pay for more family time.[16] Contrary to popular belief, most men want to be good fathers.[17] In fact, the majority of men enter marriage dreaming about positive family relationships with their future children. For example, in one study, family researchers discovered that 74 percent of men would rather have a "daddy-track" job than a "fast-track" job.[18] Happiness does indeed come from family life, and most men understand that.[19] In one study, men who engaged with their families more than their work experienced a higher quality of life compared to those who spent most of their time focused on work.[20]

Families do matter, and most American fathers are committed to their families.[21] It is somewhat paradoxical, however, that although most fathers consider family life valuable and worthwhile, oftentimes their laptops receive more "hands-on" time than their children. Unfortunately, many contemporary fathers have found it too easy to neglect their families.

Not only do families matter, but research repeatedly documents that fathers also matter. In his landmark book *Life without Father*, author David Popenoe concluded, "I know of few other bodies of evidence whose weight leans so much in one direction as does the evidence about family structure: On the whole, two parents—a father and mother—are better for the child than one parent."[22] Other experts have documented that a father's involvement in a child's life influences three key outcomes: economic security, educational attainment, and the avoidance of delinquency.[23] From a gospel perspective, Latter-day Saints understand that a loving, caring, involved father can affect his children physically, emotionally, intellectually, and spiritually as well. The influence of a strong father in the lives of his children is unmeasurable.

Where Have the Heroes Gone?

Unfortunately, there is certainly a dearth of fatherhood role models in our country. Not long ago, men did not have to look very far for paternal examples. Role models could be found in the home, community, and media. It could be argued that since April of 1992, when *The Cosby Show* went off the air, television has not provided a nurturing father role model.

Since then, father bashing has been in season. Fathers have been depicted in media circles, special interest groups, and on prime-time television as *unfit* and *inadequate* at best. The most predominant way of thinking about fathering is that it is a social role which men usually perform awkwardly. For example, contemporary prime-time television portrays these "doofus dads" as troubled, deranged, pudgy, generally incompetent, and not terribly bright.[24]

Where can men look for fatherhood role models? With such a shortage of fatherhood examples, men have fewer and fewer places to turn. In the *Father Attitudes Survey*, 74 percent of the respondents looked at *other* fathers or men as examples and resources to improve their fathering. Ironically, only 62 percent looked at their *own* fathers as examples.[25] President Spencer W. Kimball helped Latter-day Saint fathers know where to look for paternal examples. Besides their own fathers and perhaps other close relations, President Kimball explained, "We all need heroes to honor and admire; we need people after whom we can pattern our lives. For us Christ is the chiefest of these. . . . Christ is our pattern, our guide, our prototype, and our friend. We seek to be like him so that we can always be with him. In a lesser degree the apostles and prophets who have lived as Christ lived also become examples for us."[26]

One such hero or role model was the man, father, and prophet— David Oman McKay. He was married to Emma Ray Riggs, and they had seven children. President McKay spoke more on marriage and family life than perhaps any other Church leader of his era. He believed actively and deeply in the family, and he lived his life in accordance with what he taught. During the 1950s and '60s, most members of the Church looked to President and Sister McKay as role models for happiness in family living. Even today, President McKay still stands as a healthy example of fatherhood. If men want to be successful fathers, they might well study the life of President McKay.

Like contemporary fathers today who work long hours and travel extensively with their jobs, David O. McKay was busier than most men of his generation. How was David O. McKay able to balance his Church life and his professional career with his family? Unlike most

David O. McKay was in his early thirties when he was called to be an Apostle and hence had a young family to tend to. (Courtesy of Church History Library.)

men who are called into the Quorum of the Twelve in the twilight of their lives, David O. McKay had young children in the home during his service in the Quorum of the Twelve and the First Presidency. As an author and researcher, I have had the privilege of reading David O. McKay's diaries and personal letters housed in the Special Collections at the University of Utah's J. Willard Marriott Library. I have discovered that he was a remarkable father, despite the fact that he traveled so extensively when his children were younger, and that so much Church responsibility was placed on his shoulders at a relatively young age. This book will attempt to demonstrate how David O. McKay connected with his children, nurtured them, loved them, and disciplined them.

We will first examine a brief history of fatherhood so that we can view David O. McKay in the proper context. It is never fair or appropriate to try to place historical figures into contemporary settings. To understand how David O. McKay operated as a father, we must look at him in the proper early twentieth-century context. For example, it was very unusual in the early 1900s for fathers to be in the delivery room when their wives gave birth to children. Today, contemporary husbands are helping deliver babies and cutting umbilical cords—a foreign practice to fathers in the McKay era. After a historical view of fatherhood, we will consider the following father strengths that David O. McKay possessed: commitment, creativity, ability to nurture and build relationships, flexibility, and discipline. Strong and effective

David O. McKay in Historical Context

"The father who, because of business or political or social responsibilities, fails to share with his wife the responsibilities of rearing his sons and daughters is untrue to his marital obligation, is a negative element in what might and should be a joyous home atmosphere, and is a possible contributor to discord and delinquency."
—David O. McKay[1]

A brief examination of the history of fatherhood in America will provide better understanding and the context for David O. McKay as a father. In discussing the evolution of fatherhood, there appears to be three instrumental time periods worth examining: the colonial and puritanical period, the enlightened and industrialized period, and the "breadwinnerhood" versus fatherhood period. Incidentally, in reviewing these three periods, it becomes apparent that fatherhood has always been primarily driven by the nation's economic situation, which will be shown hereafter.

The 1700s: Colonial and Puritan Fatherhood

During the 1700s, the role of the American father was distinct. He was the head of the household, the unquestioned ruler: stern, rigid, and authoritative.[2] Moreover, he was the preeminent teacher of religion, morals, and values in the home. In fact, "a man who neglected the educational and religious life of his children disqualified himself as a good father. Nor could a good father leave the discipline of children to his less trusted, more pliant and emotional wife."[3] It appeared that the father ruled the roost while his wife assisted him as was needed or requested. Interestingly, during this time period, parenting books were directed toward the father because he was considered the primary parent—not the mother. Not only were men the chief educators in their homes, but they were also the prime public educators as well. The entire school system was taught and administered by men.

Furthermore, since the Puritan father was agrarian, he was a "stay-home" dad—making a living on the farm. The colonial father was a man who essentially worked from home. As such, this father spent a great deal of time with his children—interacting with them by reading, studying, working, and playing. Consequently, his influence was directly felt by his children as most of his day was spent in their presence.

The colonial father deeply valued his children and home life. Even so, colonial fathers were not characterized as having open or affectionate affiliations with their offspring.[4] In fact, the parent-child relationship of this period can certainly be characterized as a *working* one—the child worked next to his or her father most of the day.[5] The father was the stern boss, and his children were essentially his employees. Regarding parenting, the father was the key player while his wife served as his assistant.

The 1800s: Enlightened and Industrialized Father

The 1800s yielded a different father. Indeed, a metamorphosis occurred as fathers were encouraged to change their temperament from stern and harsh to more tenderhearted and empathetic. This time period also became known as the age of industrialization and urbanization. As families began to migrate from the country to the cities, the fathers' prime responsibility was altered dramatically. Family scholar David Popenoe further explained: "As income-producing work left the home, so—during the weekday—did the men. Men increasingly withdrew from direct-care parenting and specialized in the provider or bread-winner role. The man's prime responsibility was to take care of his families economic needs. . . . For the first time in history on a large scale, women filled the roles of mother and housewife full-time."[6]

However, men were still viewed as the head of the home, but they were now becoming assistants to their wives instead of the other way around.[7] The roles of men and women were changing during this period of enlightenment and industrialization. Perhaps some of these changes were constructive and beneficial. After all, it seemed that men and women were becoming more complete as their assets and liabilities flowed together into a *joint* marriage account. Men were taking upon them some feminine qualities, and women were assuming a more masculine posture in the home. After all things were considered, this shift seemed like a good idea.

However, the experts contended that such changes were *not* healthy for the society. For example, Stephen M. Frank argued, "As some fathers began to spend more time at work and less time at home, and as family structure shifted away from patriarchal dominance and toward more companionate relationships, paternal requirements shrank."[8] Simply put, relationships at home were certainly more affable, but the role of father was diminishing.[9] In fact, 1842 was the year a New England pastor warned that paternal neglect was causing "the ruin of many families."[10] So, as men began to gradually slip out of their children's lives, parenting books and child-rearing manuals began to focus on mothers; after all, they were the ones who were now raising the children.

However, not all fathers at this juncture were deadbeats. There were some men, perhaps many, who were enjoying their fathering role during this time in our nation's history. These fathers were making time for their children. Toys, books, games, children's names, and even home structure reflected a newfound love for children and parenting.[11] Other evidence suggests that fathers enjoyed playing with their children, "lamented separation from them, frequently gave them gifts, worried about their health, celebrated their accomplishments, and looked after their academic preparation."[12]

The 1900s: Breadwinners Versus Fathers

By the turn of the twentieth century, the role of the father changed again. A good father was now defined as one who helped his wife. Masculinity was redefined, and male toughness became a major theme.

Traits such as competitiveness, assertiveness, and "virility" became desirable. Popenoe reported: "This shift in the definition of masculinity—away from family protector-provider towards expressive individualism—was damaging to fatherhood. A locker-room mentality among young males was growing. Male excitement and adventure were emphasized, and masculine humor grew disparaging of marriage and family responsibility. Children were increasingly left out of the male equation. More men were leaving their families."[13]

Thus, men took a step from patriarchy to individualism. Most men were too arrogant to become "second fiddle" in domestic duties. Therefore, many fathers dropped out of the home-life picture altogether. Although David O. McKay lived during this time period, he appears to be the exception rather than the rule when it comes to involved fathers. Yes, President McKay was busy, but he was an involved father. Not only was he nurturing, but he made time for his children. He had a strong personal connection with each of his children; consequently, he had a strong influence in the lives of each of his children.

For example, in the April general conference of 1967, President McKay's son Robert spoke in the priesthood meeting. During the late '60s, President McKay had become too ill to speak in general conference; therefore, his sons would most often read his prepared messages to the general Church membership. However, this message was somewhat different because Robert actually shared a brief message before delivering his father's remarks. He said:

> Brethren, I think there isn't a son among you here who would pass this opportunity in the presence of about 95,000 brethren to tell your father how much you loved him. The question comes to me frequently, as it does to my brothers, "How does it feel to be the son of a prophet?" How do you answer a question like that? You don't explain it; you live it.
>
> As my father, he has my love and devotion, and I echo the thoughts of my brothers and sisters. As the President of the Church, and as a prophet of our Heavenly Father, he has my obedience as a member of the priesthood, and my sustaining vote.
>
> I can say this, and act as a personal witness, because in all of my years of close association in the home, on the farm, in business, in the

Church, there has never been shown to me one action nor one word, even while training a self-willed horse, which would throw any doubt in my mind that he should be and finally did become the representative and prophet of our Heavenly Father. I leave you that personal witness, and I will close that in the name of Jesus Christ. Amen.[14]

It is not hard to detect in this message Robert's love, respect, and adoration for his father. The fact that he never witnessed his father act in any way that was not in harmony with the behavior of a prophet of God is a powerful statement. Because of David O. McKay's great love for his children, he was able to have a strong impact on their lives. As an aged prophet, he reaped the dividends that came from an investment he made years earlier—spending time with his children.

1900 to the 1930s

This time period marks perfectly the fatherhood period of David O. McKay. Each of his seven children was born between 1900 and 1930. During this time, the role of the American father had become clear-cut: the man's primary duty was to be the family breadwinner. Instead of being defined in terms of moral teaching and patriarchy, successful fathers became men who could "bring home the bacon."[15] Consequently, the family lost its stability, structure, popularity, and power. The national birthrate dropped from 7 children per family in 1800 to 3.56 in 1900.[16]

America was in trouble, and many fingers began pointing toward fathers. An article appeared in the 7 July 1932 issue of *Parents Magazine* entitled "For Fathers Only," which seemed to identify the core of the crisis. The article labeled contemporary teenagers as "the generation of woman-raised youth" and concluded with this statement: "Perhaps the answer to the frequent question, 'What's wrong with modern youth?' is simply, 'It is fatherless.'"[17] The article might have been premature, but the point was well made: if fathers did not reassume their role and become more involved with their families, the nation would be in deep and serious trouble.

Men began to redefine their paternal role by the cohort they associated with on an everyday basis—their working peer group. Perhaps as men commenced to work in the factories, the role of father lost its salience. It appears that men interacted and bonded with other men and subsequently did not need their families, nor did they see themselves any longer as *family men*. David Blankenhorn made his mark in the 1990s by defending fatherhood and substantiating the need for men in families. He is the author of *Fatherless America* and *The Future of Marriage*. From his research on fathers, Blankenhorn substantiated his claim that during this time period, more and more men "looked outside the home for the meaning of their maleness. Masculinity became less domesticated, defined less by effective paternity and more by individual ambition and achievement. Fatherhood became a thinner social role. . . . Paternal authority declined as the fatherhood script came to be anchored in, and restricted to, two paternal tasks: head of the family and breadwinner."[18]

Perhaps the ultimate blow to fatherhood was the Great Depression. By the 1930s, fatherhood meant breadwinning. The American perception was that income level determined paternal success. Therefore, "the Depression shattered the identities of millions of men as fathers and breadwinners."[22] Some men became depressed and suicidal because they could no longer provide for their families. Although some would argue that unemployment would bring a father closer to his children (since he would have more spare time), just the opposite proved to be true. The Great Depression actually forced family men to devote their attention to finding jobs and placed much strain on those who were already working. In many cases, fathers were forced to leave their homes and venture into distant cities to find work. Ultimately, children were dropped from their father's calendar.

Home, then, became the scene of a man's failure: "His children were a daily reminder that he had failed at the fundamental task of fatherhood, which left him consumed by guilt and a profound sense of inadequacy."[19] So fathers stayed away from the very place they were needed the most—the home. As fathers neglected their families, they subsequently lost their identity while children and mothers suffered the consequences.[20]

David O. McKay viewed himself as more than a mere breadwinner. He was involved as a parent and took his paternal responsibility

The Quorum of the Twelve Apostles in 1931. (Courtesy of Intellectual Reserve, Inc.)

seriously. Even so, he still had to balance his roles as husband, father, provider, and church leader. He was an educator by trade; therefore, funds were often tight. Besides breadwinning, David also bore the heavy load of Church responsibilities. By the cultural standards during the early 1900s, David was not expected to be a nurturing father. As we explore his life, we will come to understand, however, that he was.

1930s to the 1950s

In some ways, World War II rescued many men who had failed as fathers. Primarily, the war provided men with an income. They could

7

now support their families as the role of breadwinner was reestablished. Emotionally, the war also assisted in restoring pride and self-worth to fathers as they left their families and went overseas to "fight for their country." During the war years, however, America became by force a "fatherless society" again. Women had to once again assume the role of mother and father. Needless to say, the war took an emotional toll on the women of America as they tried to hold their families together.

Soon after the 1940s, however, the tides appeared to change as men came home and assumed their patriarchal roles. For the most part, families were excited to have dad home. However, for many families, it was a "rough entry," as the father had to find his way back into the family. After all, mothers had things running rather smoothly for the last few years. Even so, with some time and patience, fatherhood was rejuvenated as America moved into the next decade.

In the 1950s, television personalities Ozzie Nelson and Ward Cleaver began to represent ideal fatherhood. Men's priorities transformed due to the damaging effects of the war; they realized what they had been missing and were anxious to reestablish their roles as nurturing fathers. Subsequently, stability was restored to the American family. Only 11 percent of children born in the 1950s saw their parents' divorce, and only 5 percent of the nation's children were born out of wedlock.[21] Robert E. Griswold, noted historian and professor at the University of Oklahoma, commented, "Fathers who went begging for work in the 1930s now had a variety of high-paying jobs from which to choose, and with work men gained a new sense of manhood."[22] Moreover, the healthy American family was what the war had been about, and almost every family scholar agreed that the traditional family, with a homebound mother and wage-earning father, would best maintain the familial stability needed to reestablish the traditional family in America. Hence, strong families could provide order and stability to the larger society, and a hearty society could provide an anchor to a war-torn world.

Children of the Depression became the fathers of the 1950s. These men wanted to make up for lost time. By doing so, they became involved and active in the lives of their children. Fathers began to assist their children with homework, coach little league, and occasionally make an appearance at a PTA meeting. It appeared that men were making recompense for their own deficits just a decade earlier and trying to redeem themselves from the "sins of their fathers."

Such a paradigm shift is useful in explaining why a 1957 study found that 63 percent of 850 fathers had a positive attitude toward parenting. As men began to reconstruct their lives, fathering provided meaning and positive interactions with their children, who reinforced the paternal role. Consequently, fathers were finding fulfillment through family life. Soon, men began to read books, listen to radio programs, and attend workshops on parenting and family life.

During this time period, David O. McKay was in the First Presidency of the Church and had children as well as grandchildren at home. He embraced a new fatherhood where men were more nurturing and involved in their children's lives. He seemed to be ahead of the curve, however, because this more kind, gentle, and involved father approach is how President McKay always did it.

David O. McKay seems to have more in common with the fathers in the '40s and '50s who were more nurturing and involved. Although it was a challenge for him to spend significant amounts of time with his children, when he was with them, he made the time count. He used the time he had with his children to teach them, to influence them, to laugh with them, and to make memories with them.

Notes

1. David O. McKay, in Conference Report, April 1965, 7.

2. David Popenoe, *Life without Father*, 87.

3. Robert L. Griswold, "Generative Fathering: A Historical Perspective," in *Generative Fathering: Beyond Deficit Perspectives*, ed. Alan J. Hawkins and David C. Dollahite (Thousand Oaks, CA: SAGE Publications, 1997), 71–86.

4. Griswold, "Generative Fathering," 72–73.

5. Two other fascinating details have been noted by researcher David Blankenhorn. He explained that "in almost all cases of divorce, it was established practice to award the custody of children to fathers. [Also] throughout this period, fathers, not mothers, were the chief correspondents with children who lived away from home." Blankenhorn, *Fatherless America: Confronting Our Most Urgent Social Problem* (New York: Basic Books, 1995), 13.

6. Popenoe, *Life without Father*, 93.

7. Furthermore, historians have documented that during this period of "enlightenment," the building blocks for a marriage were no longer economically centered, but now focused on intimacy and romance. That is to say, during the 1700s (colonial or Puritan fatherhood), mate selection was based on assets and potential for economic production; thus, the marriage relationship was often considered cold and distant. However, during the 1800s, the situation changed and marital relations were built on love, trust, and even sexuality. Robert L. Griswold, *Fatherhood in America: A History* (New York: Basic Books, 1993).

8. Blankenhorn, *Fatherless America*, 14.

9. J. H. Pleck, "American Fathering in Historical Perspective," in *Changing Men: New Directions in Research on Men and Masculinity*, ed. Michael S. Kimmel (Newbury Park, CA: SAGE Publications, 1987), 86.

10. Blankenhorn, *Fatherless America*, 14.

11. For example, Isaac Avery's pride in his son, just four months old, was manifest in a letter to a friend: "Thomas Lenoir Avery, a young gentlemen . . . can sit alone, laugh out loud and cut other smart capers for a fellow of his age and is the handsomest of all [our] . . . children." See Griswold, *Fatherhood in America*, 18.

12. Griswold, "Generative Fathering," 73–74.

13. Popenoe, *Life without Father*, 112.

14. Robert R. McKay, in Conference Report, April 1967, 84.

15. Michael E. Lamb, "The History of Research on Father Involvement: An Overview," *Marriage and Family Review* 29, no. 2–3 (2000): 23–42.

16. President Theodore Roosevelt immediately warned the country about "race suicide." Equally alarming was the divorce rate: from 1900 to 1920 it increased 100 percent. See Popenoe, *Life without Father*, 115.

17. Griswold, *Fatherhood in America*, 95.

18. Blankenhorn, *Fatherless America*, 15.

19. Griswold, *Fatherhood in America*, 44.

20. The "fatherless" generation of the 1930s produced a generation of deficient men and delinquent children—many fathers left their "homes in disgrace while their delinquent children gathered on street corners looking for trouble." See Griswold, *Fatherhood in America*, 146.

21. Barbara Defoe Whitehead, "Dan Quayle Was Right," *Atlantic Monthly*, April 1993, 47–84.

22. Griswold, *Fatherhood in America*, 162.

2

Committed Father

"Fatherhood is leadership, the most important kind of leadership. It has always been so; it always will be so. Father, with the assistance and counsel and encouragement of your eternal companion, you preside in the home."[1]
—David O. McKay

The late Dr. Paul Pearsall, neuropsychologist, author, and popular lecturer admonished to all parents, "I warn you that if your family does not come first, your family will not last."[2] Strong fathers understand that their family must top their priority list, regardless of other responsibilities. Committed fathers dedicate their time, talents, and resources to building and strengthening their families. Besides being willing to make sacrifices, committed fathers are involved, available, and accessible. *They put their family first.* Unfortunately, we live in an age where there are many distractions that compete for our time. For example, consider the television. Unlike a generation ago when most families had access to three channels, today there are literally thousands of channels to choose from. The average American family has their television set on approximately seven hours per day.[3] One study documented that American men spend fifteen hours per week watching television, while women spend almost seventeen hours per week in front of the tube.[4]

Other media sources that compete for our time include computers, the Internet, music, social media, cell phones, text messages, video games, and Netflix. Many American men spend inordinate amounts of time on their smartphones, surfing the Internet and playing video games. According to a recent Nielsen survey, men between the ages of eighteen and thirty-four are the most prevalent users of video games, with 48 percent of men using a video console each day, averaging 2.5 hours daily.[5] No wonder family expert Dr. William Doherty warned, "The more we wire our houses, the less we connect with one another in our families."[6]

However, being "wired" is only part of the problem. Many children today are overscheduled with competitive sports, club teams, tournaments, lessons, friends, parties, school activities, games, and performances. Not that any of these activities are bad, but too many activities can cause both children and parents much unwanted stress. It seems that life has become more complex than it probably should be. In fact, some modern parents feel that their children are busier than they are. Being busy has become the new status symbol, and the trophies now go to the busiest.[7]

With all of the contemporary distractions, a father's commitment will be challenged, or at least interfered with. If fathers are to be effective, they must have clear priorities. Their family must come first in their lives. If we were to survey one thousand Latter-day Saint fathers and ask them, "What is the most important thing in your life?" it seems safe to assume that over 98 percent would say, "Family." That is a very popular answer. However, there is often incongruence between what we say and what we actually do. For example, if we were to ask those one thousand Latter-day Saint fathers in our imaginary survey, "So, if your family is so important, how much time did you spend with your family this week? Last week? Yesterday? Last night?" it is possible that the percentage that would report significant time spent would drop drastically. Being a committed father requires more than mere lip service. Many of us will say that our family is our first priority. However, our priorities are determined by where we spend our time— not necessarily by what we verbalize. Dr. Stephen R. Covey—educator, author, and consultant—taught, "If you really want to prioritize your family, you simply have to plan ahead and be strong. It's not enough to say your family is important. If 'family' is really going to be top priority, you have to 'hunker down, suck it up, and make it happen!'"[8]

To be a committed father is to literally bind ourselves to our children in a relationship.[9] Commitment is the foundation stone on which successful fatherhood rests. Without commitment, there is no influence or effectiveness in fathering. Research from the National Study of Families and Households revealed that when fathers are committed and engaged, their children experience fewer behavioral problems and anxieties, get along well with others, and are much more responsible when compared to children who have fathers that are not committed or involved.[10]

Marriage Is the First Commitment

For a father, the first point of commitment in family life is to the marriage. Roman statesman Marcus Tullius Cicero said, "The first bond of society is marriage."[11] Not only is marriage the first bond of society but it is certainly the prime relationship in a family. As the marriage goes, the family is sure to follow. It would be difficult for any father to be successful without a strong marriage relationship. As even the most casual Church historian will know that David O. McKay had a solid relationship with his wife, Emma Ray. Latter-day Saints who lived during President McKay's tenure as the President of the Church were eyewitnesses to the love that this couple publicly demonstrated to each other. It was President McKay who taught, "A father can do no greater thing for his children than to let them feel that he loves their mother."[12]

It was clear that President McKay loved Emma Ray and wished to be with her as often as possible. When he had to travel, he would attempt to take her with him any chance he could. Early in their marriage, when David served in the Weber Stake Sunday School superintendency, she would travel many miles with him in a horse-drawn buggy in the open air, holding their baby on her lap. All this was done so that she and David could spend time together. She once confided in a friend, "I have a husband who wants me to be with him, and I'm glad to do what he wants me to do."[13] And when David was required to travel alone as an Apostle, his letters to Emma Ray were filled with his deep love, loyalty,

David O. McKay and wife, Emma Ray. (Courtesy of Intellectual Reserve, Inc.)

and commitment. He was constantly pledging his love, support, and admiration. He would often assure her, "My soul is with you."[14]

Perhaps there is no more poignant tribute than the letter he wrote to all of his children, dated 25 October 1934, just after David was called into the First Presidency of the Church. In the letter, he gave every ounce of credit for his new calling to Emma Ray. He wrote of her:

> Willingly and ably she has carried the responsibility of the household.
>
> Uncomplainingly she has economized when our means have been limited—and that has been the case nearly all our lives.
>
> Always prompt with meals, she has never said an unpleasant word or even shown a frown when I have kept her waiting, sometimes for hours.
>
> If I had to take a train at midnight or later, she would either sit up with me or lie awake to make sure that I should not over sleep.
>
> If duty required me to leave at five o'clock in the morning, she was never satisfied unless she could prepare me a bite of breakfast before I left home.

It has been mother who remembered the birthdays and purchased the Christmas presents.

Since January 2nd, 1901, the happy day when she became my bride, she has never given me a single worry except when she was ill and that has been, with few exceptions, only with the responsibilities of motherhood. . . .

Sometimes I have come home tired and irritable and have made remarks provocative of retaliating replies; but never to this day have you heard your mother say a cross or disrespectful word. This can be said truthfully I think of but a few women in the world. . . .

To her we owe our happy family life and whatever success we may have achieved.

I know you love her and, oh how she loves each one of you![15]

Without question, the children in the McKay family were the beneficiaries and the witnesses of their parents' strong and happy marriage. The strength and commitment of their marriage carried over into David's role as a father. His strong relationship with Emma Ray gave him the power, wisdom, confidence, and fortitude to be an effective parent.

Generally speaking, a father can demonstrate his commitment by investing much of his time and energy to family life. Being committed to the family implies staying steadfast, enduring trials, remaining sexually loyal in the marital union, sacrificing, giving the most to those who matter most, and having common goals. Basically, commitment means that the family comes first. Throughout his life as a parent, David O. McKay not only demonstrated his commitment to his own children but to other children as well.

Family First

David O. McKay was always an extremely busy man. From the time he graduated from college and began teaching at the Weber Academy, he seemed to travel at Mach speed. His life was full with his teaching career, Church duties, farm responsibilities, and a young, growing family. He married Emma Ray Riggs on 2 January 1901 at the age of twenty-seven. Before they had been married a year, on 30 September 1901, Emma Ray gave birth to their first child, David Lawrence McKay.[16] Not long after Lawrence's birth, David had a Church meeting to attend to. He had been called as the second assistant to Thomas B. Evans, the Weber Stake Sunday School's superintendent. The McKays' first major quarrel occurred when David was leaving to attend the meeting. "As he started to put on his hat and coat, Ray had thought, 'Surely you aren't going to a meeting tonight.' As if reading her thoughts, David turned and looked at her for a moment, and said, 'Have you forgotten that it is Sunday School Board Meeting tonight?' There was no warmth in her kiss as she bade him good-bye. The closing door wakened the baby. Still weak, she sat and rocked the crying baby while tears of weakness, frustrations, and hurt welled down her cheeks." Emma Ray decided that scene would not be repeated, and the McKays learned to balance family and busy schedules.[17]

Like all new parents, adjustments would need to be made, and sacrifices on the part of both parents would be offered. David would also have to learn to adjust his priorities. After all, he would be the one to later quote J. E. McCullough's famous statement: "No other success can compensate for failure in the home."[18] David would eventually discover that being a righteous father was actually much more important than attending to his Church duties.[19] He would also come to understand that to be an effective father, he would have to be present at home. Elder Harold B. Lee taught:

> Sometimes as I go throughout the Church, I think I am seeing a man who is using his church work as a kind of escape from family responsibility. And sometimes when we've talked about whether or not he's giving attention to his family, his children and his wife, he says something like this: "Well, I'm so busy taking care of the Lord's work that I really don't have time." And I say to him, "My dear brother, the greatest of the Lord's work that you and I will ever do is the work that we do within the walls of our own home." Now don't you get any misconception about where the Lord's work starts. That's the most important of all the Lord's work. And you wives may have to remind your husbands of that occasionally.[20]

Like most fathers, David would come to learn the balance between Church work and family work. He would also learn to recognize that the most important of the Lord's work he would ever do were within the walls of his own home. Ultimately, Emma Ray and the children came to believe that they were most important in David's life. But this endeavor would take time.

A Busy Schedule

When he was called to the Quorum of the Twelve Apostles in April of 1906 at the age of thirty-two, he and Emma Ray were seasoned adults and mature beyond their years.[21] Nevertheless, their family was quite young. At the time of his call to the Quorum of the Twelve, they had two children under the age of five, and they were soon expecting a third.[22] Moreover, when David was called into the Quorum of the Twelve, he maintained his position as principal of the Weber Academy for two more years. Therefore, David would work a full day at the academy and then catch a train in the middle of the afternoon to head to Salt Lake City to work as an Apostle. He would often return home to Ogden around midnight or shortly after. Then he would wake up the next day before 5:00 a.m. and begin the entire routine again. On a typical day, his schedule could look like the following:

> 7:45 Rhetoric class
> 8:40 Faculty prayer meeting
> 8:45 Devotional
> 9:15 Theology class
> 10:30 English class
> 11:20 General school work
> 12:10 Dinner
> 1:15 Board train for SLC
> 2:30 Committee meeting
> 3:30 Special Sunday School work
> 5:30 Committee arrangements
> 7:00 General Sunday School board meeting

11:45 Board train home for Ogden

1:30 a.m. Retire[23]

Sometimes, David would be so tired that he would actually secure a hotel in Salt Lake City late at night in order to rest.[24] Unlike most busy fathers today, David didn't have weekends to recover from the weekly grind. Instead, he fulfilled his duty as an Apostle, visiting stake conferences all throughout the United States. Sometimes, his apostolic assignment would require him to be gone for weeks at a time. This was a huge challenge for such a young family. In one account, he reported, "Returned home at midnight and met Ray for the first time in two days."[25] After one long trip, David returned home and complimented Emma Ray on a wonderful evening dinner. His daughter Lou Jean, who was four years old at the time, spoke up and said to her father, "Come again sometime."[26] Even his children understood that their father simply was not home much.

Single Parenthood

Consequently, Emma Ray became the primary parent, and the lion's share of the family load fell upon her.[27] Besides being a "single mother" who was burdened with the responsibility of raising seven children with their father away most of the time, Emma Ray was also David's personal secretary. While David was away on Church business, he asked Emma Ray in many of his personal letters to take care of some of his business affairs at the Weber Academy. For example, in a letter dated 8 June 1907, written from St. George, David asks Emma Ray to go to his office at the academy, get an address out of his desk drawer, and craft a letter to a woman who had applied for a teaching position, telling her the position had been filled.[28] In many of his personal letters to Emma Ray, it is not unusual to find instances of David asking her to take care of Church-related issues, make phone calls, submit manuscripts, transact academy business, or even meddle with farm business while he was away.[29]

David recognized the additional weight Emma Ray was carrying, and he often worried about her health and her ability to deal with the added pressures. In a letter to his beloved wife, he closed, "Ray, dearest, the Lord bless you and keep you always, and strengthen you in carrying the added responsibility that comes to you because of my continual absence from your side!"[30] He prayed to the Lord that she would become equal to the tasks and responsibilities they both had been given.

The double burden of being a single parent and a private secretary made Emma Ray just as busy, if not busier, than her husband. Nevertheless, Emma Ray bore the responsibility well. She enjoyed motherhood and seemed to have a great time with her children. Lawrence described his mother's taxing load and her good nature:

> So it was Mother who had much of the responsibility of rearing the family. Mother was the one who taught us all to pray at our bedsides and to rely on our Father in Heaven. It was mother who told us we couldn't play baseball on Sunday. She was a great companion. There was no generation gap. She went to movies with us; she enjoyed John Bunny and Fatty Arbuckle as much as we did, and finally convinced Father that there was humor in a Mack Sennett comedy. She read good literature to us and told us stories and sang to us at night. . . . She loved games, too. Rook, Pit, and backgammon were popular in our home. Father often joined us in evenings of fun.[31]

No wonder David O. McKay later taught, "By nature the true mother is self-sacrificing. She is ever giving something of her life to make another either happier or better. Dying and giving—giving and dying—the two great elements that make the truly heroic—these are the Christian virtues that make motherhood sublime."[32] David must have had Emma Ray in mind when he stated these words.

Family State of Mind

Although David O. McKay was an extremely busy man, his commitment to his family never wavered. Just because David was away from home so often should not imply that he was an absentee father. Of course, he wasn't home physically, but emotionally he was present.

Many of his personal letters to Emma Ray reflect that his family was constantly on his mind while he traveled, especially on those long train rides to stake conferences. In a letter he wrote on a train in southeastern Arizona, he said, "I pray constantly that you and our little ones will be kept in health and happiness. The strongest desire of my life is to have a pure, happy home—and ideal family."[33]

He closed many of his letters with phrases like "love and kisses to you and the boys,"[34] "thinking of you and the babes,"[35] or "how are the boys and the baby?"[36] In many of David's letters to Emma Ray, he would go into more detail about his concern for the children. For instance, in a letter dated 27 July 1907, written from what David referred to as "Nearly off the earth," which was somewhere near Durango, Colorado, he wrote, "Physically, I am over a thousand miles away from you, but there is not an hour [that] passes without my seeing every one of you in our lovely home. My soul is with you. When in imagination I hear those little ones coughing, and see your worry, my whole being is wrung in sympathy."[37]

There are indications that David wanted to be home more often and perhaps felt guilty that he was gone as much as he was. On 6 February 1907, speaking of his family, he wrote in his diary, "I feel that I am away from them too often."[38] He seemed to covet more time with his family, and wished he had more resources to do fun things with his children. In another letter, dated 13 March 1909, from somewhere near Rawlins, Wyoming, David wrote:

> My Dearest Sweetheart:
>
> I am wishing we had money—a pile of it. And I have wished so continually nearly all day. Lonesomeness has produced the wish—a longing lonesomeness that only one can dispel, and she my sweetheart—Ray. I have been thinking that if we had a large income, you and the babes and a girl to take care of them in hotels could all go with me on these little trips. Then I could attend to my duties, and be at home also; for home is anywhere if loved ones be there.
>
> Well, we have not money, so we can go together only occasionally. Such trips, then, become oasis and trips like this today, sandy deserts. . . .

Yes, I wish for money, but not because I don't feel rich. With you and the boys, and "papa's tomboy"— "papa's girl" and our happy home surroundings, with papa still with us, . . . with the bright prospects in life, and our membership in the Church—with all this wealth and more, I feel the richest man in the world! But I wish you were with me just the same.

Lovingly,

Your own Dade

xxx Kisses to Lawrence, Llewelyn, and Lou Jean[39]

In another letter from St. Johns, Arizona, David wrote, "O if I could only step in the dear old dining room tonight—just long enough to carry my boys on my 'Sodjers' [shoulders], kiss them and Lou Jean good night; and then sit down with my sweetheart—on my knee and her soft arm around my neck, and talk over our blessings, our duties, or visits, or even our debts, how happy I should be!"[40]

Therefore, when David arrived home from his travels, he made his time count. He would attempt to spend as much time with his family as he possibly could. Moreover, if he could share or remove some of the constant burden that Emma Ray felt, he tried to do so. His diaries from 1908 capture how he treasured his rare and precious time with his precious ones: Wednesday, 1 January 1908: "Spent the first day of the year with my family at home"[41]; Sunday, 31 May, 1908: "Spent this day of rest with my family"[42]; Friday, 10 July 1908: "Took the children to Huntsville . . . Returned home in the evening"[43]; Tuesday, 3 November 1908: "Spent the day with Ray and the babes"[44]; and Friday, 25 December 1908: "At home all day. Spent a happy time with the children."[45]

He Would Rather Be Home

When some members of the Church read and study the travels of David O. McKay, they may become jealous. Perhaps they too wish they could travel and see the world, as did this young Apostle. If given the choice, however, David would have rather been home with his family than traveling the world. In fact, leaving home for long periods of time was an extremely difficult task for him.

David, along with Hugh J. Cannon, went on a world tour from 1920 to 1921. David understood how difficult it would be to leave his young family for such a long time. He worried about Emma Ray, the children, and even their animals! On the day he left, he wrote in his diary:

> Saturday, December 4th, 1920: A telephone call at 6:30 a.m. from my Scotch friend and brother, William Kenly, who just wanted to say good bye, started me out with the full realization that this would be my last day with my loved ones for perhaps eight or ten months—probably longer. As the morning hours lengthened into day, this realization became more intense and my feelings more tender. The press of packing and attending to a hundred eleventh hour duties proved to be a good channel into which my thoughts and feelings were diverted. . . .
>
> Parting from those we love is never an easy task; but today it seemed more difficult than ever. Every little household duty when performed seemed to say, this is the last time for a while; even the fire in the furnace looked gloomy when I threw in the last shovelful of coal.
>
> However, I kept my feelings pretty well under control until I began to say good bye to the children. Baby thinking I was going to coo to him looked up and gave me his sweetest smile. The beautiful, innocent radiance of his baby face will be a treasured memory all during my missionary tour.
>
> Then came Ned, my sleeping companion and affectionate tender boy. He couldn't realize why his daddy was sobbing. His tear dimmed eyes and inquiring expression revealed the emotion in his little soul! What a blessing that it would be but transient in his childish nature!
>
> The parting moment with my Sweetheart and true devoted wife, my life's companion and Joy, I cannot describe. Such sacred scenes, anyhow, are not for expression in words—they find expression only in the depths of a loving soul.

Emma Ray, Lou Jean, and Llewelyn accompanied me to the train—Emma Ray, the Sunbeam; Lou Jean, the Rosebud; and Llewelyn, the Leader, who in his young manhood, in the absence of his brother and father, must assume all the duties of the farm and the household heretofore carried by the three of us. No father can be prouder of his children than I, nor more confident of their fidelity and desire for success. Parting from them at the station stirred my feelings wholly beyond control. I left them, though, having the comforting assurance that each would be a sweetheart to Mama and life for her comfort and pleasure.[46]

These words leave little doubt that it was simply heart-wrenching for David to leave his wife and children for this extended period of time. To add insult to injury, he departed on this journey the first week of December, just as the Christmas season was ramping up into full gear. To be away from his family during Christmas would be especially difficult. The next day, 5 December, he wrote in his diary, "Any thought of Christmas this year makes me homesick."[47]

Once on the ship, his homesickness continued. He wrote, "There are more babies and children on this vessel than there were on [the previous ship he was on], but they keep their nurses and mamas pretty busy. After all, babies are better off at home. And so are their Daddies!"[48] Obviously, as a father himself, David would have preferred home life to cruising the Pacific.[49]

On another occasion, after a long trip to eastern Canada, he once wrote to Emma Ray, "You need not send any letters after you receive this, as I shall be somewhere on my way home—Home! Blessed haven of happiness and contentment! I would not exchange our ties of companionship and true affection for each other, our ideals as exemplified in the lives of our children, for all else this old world can offer!"[50]

In March of 1921, David was able to come home from the world tour for a short respite. It was his good fortune to be home for a period of two weeks before he had to leave again. Therefore, he viewed time with his family as precious. He wrote in his diary: "I'm glad to have had the privilege of spending these last two weeks at home, even though nine-tenths of my time has been given to the public, and only one-tenth to my family. Even the one-tenth made matters a little easier, I think, for Ray, who is worrying considerably over our perplexing financial difficulties. Old 2071 Madison is a plain, old-fashioned house, but with the sweetest wife and the dearest kiddies in the world, living in there, it is a Paradise to Me!"[51]

David O. McKay's paradise is comparable to George Bailey's (from *It's a Wonderful Life*) feelings about Bedford Falls! Despite financial troubles or other challenges, David's home in Ogden, complete with a wonderful wife and happy children, was a utopic delight—especially when compared to his global travel schedule and sleeping in a different bed as often as he did. Consequently, David learned to appreciate his home life more than most. He did not take his wife and children for granted. And when he was home, *he was home*. And when he was away, he wanted to be home![52] David would have understood the truth of a statement made by President Boyd K. Packer. After traveling the world and visiting many exotic places, President Packer was asked if he could travel to any place in the world, where would he go? He replied, "I would go home."[53] David, too, wanted to be home as often as he could, and it broke his heart that he had to be away as often as he did.

Home Sweet Home

Despite his travels, there were many periods of his life when David was home. When on his "home turf," he could demonstrate his commitment as a father by his actual presence and the decisions he made as the leader of the home. For example, on one occasion, when Llewelyn was the student body president at Weber Normal College, an idea was formulated to place a steel flagpole on the top of Mount Ogden. Llewelyn discussed the proposal with the school president, Aaron W. Tracy, and received permission to hike the entire student body to the top of the mountain to install the flagpole. Because of his great respect for his father, Llewelyn asked him, "What do you think of the idea of placing a flagpole on the top of Mount Ogden, and thereby initiating an annual trek by the whole student body to unfurl 'Old Glory' there?" David responded to his son, "It seems like quite an undertaking to haul sections of a steel pole besides cement, sand, water, and other necessary equipment to the top of that mountain, but if the administration is behind the project and the students are enthusiastic, I am sure it can be done successfully."

After all the plans were laid out, the assignments were made, and the specific details of how to hike over one thousand students to the top of a mountain were set forth, the editor of the school newspaper resigned. This was a huge disappointment for Llewelyn. It was through the school newspaper that all the instructions were to be communicated for the hike, not to mention to light a figurative fire in the hearts of the students to get them excited for the project. So much depended on the school newspaper! Llewelyn was crushed. That night at dinner, David noticed his son's downcast countenance. He asked,

"What's the matter, you act as if you had lost your last friend?" I told him of my predicament and my fear that I would have to give up my objective relative to the Mount Ogden trek.

"Never give up, my boy," he said, "difficulties will always come in your way. With the help of your classmates put the paper out yourself. You know . . . ," and a twinkle was in his eye, "I rather look forward to going with you to participate in the event!"

That was all I needed. The next day I rounded up my best friends, and we got busy writing the needed edition of the paper. We even put the resigned editor's name in it, hoping that it would encourage him to come back on the job for the following issue; and this turned out to be the case.

I think every riding horse from all surrounding towns was brought in for the occasion, and the hundreds of students who could not obtain horses hiked to the top of the mountain, led by Dr. Lind.

How happy I was when the signatures of the faculty and of the student officers were added to a document which was placed in a bottle and sealed in the cement at the bottom of the flagpole, because father's name headed the list. At that moment I came to the realization that had father not stated: "I'll take part with you," I would have given up the venture.

> The flagpole still stands on the top of Mount Ogden. It is nothing more than a steel flagpole to many people, but to me it is a symbol of how important are a few appropriate words of a father to his son, and especially of how significant is the encouraging statement: "I'll go along with you!"[54]

Without question, here is an example of a father who was committed to his son. He was also committed to his son's success.[55] David O. McKay was willing to put his son before his own needs and schedule. Because of his father's influence in the Ogden area, not to mention the entire Church, Llewelyn was able to carry out a task that seemed insurmountable. Not only that, but he also learned of his father's unwavering support and commitment. From that moment on, Llewelyn knew that regardless of how "unimportant" something in his life was to the rest of the world, his father would always be there to show his love and support.

Surrogate Father

David O. McKay was not only committed to his own family but his commitment was to all youth of the next generation. Strong fathers are not only committed to their own children but to nieces, nephews, neighbors, friends, fellow ward members, and citizens of the community.[56] Aaron W. Tracy, who was mentioned previously in this work, was the president of Weber Normal College when Llewelyn was the student body president. However, years earlier, Aaron was on the verge of dropping out of school because of his financial situation.

He approached President McKay, who at the time was the president of Weber Academy, and related to him his plight. He said, "President McKay, it looks as if I shall have to withdraw from school for a while, for I am unable to make ends meet financially. I shall return again later, however, because I am determined to get an education. For the time being, I shall have to find full-time work." David learned that Aaron was an orphaned boy who lived alone in a small back room of someone's home. He walked miles to school each day and provided his own food, clothing, and tuition costs by accepting odd jobs. Sensing

Aaron's concern and perhaps realizing his potential, David said, "My boy . . . you are absolutely right in wanting an education, and if you are determined to continue until graduation, let us see if we can't work something out. Now my wife needs someone to help out around the house, and we have a spare room upstairs in our home where you can sleep and thus save room rent. Why don't you move in with us?"[57]

Llewelyn reported that Aaron was grateful for the opportunity. He moved into the McKay home the next day and became part of the family. He helped Sister McKay with the household chores during the week, and, on weekends and in the summer time, he worked on the McKay farm in Huntsville. David would say of him, "I like that boy; he always does the job right. He is determined to make good; you mark my word, he will reach his goal with such determination." Aaron did reach his goal. As he attended classes at the academy, under the tutelage of master teacher David O. McKay, he decided that he wanted to become a teacher himself. After graduation from Weber, he continued his schooling. Years later, he became the president of Weber Normal College. Aaron Tracy was remembered by his students as one of the great teachers of the college.[58]

Aaron wasn't the only student who reaped the benefits of David O. McKay's kindness and commitment to the youth of the Church. His daughter Jeanette McKay Morrell reported, "Besides rearing and educating their own family, the McKays invited many students to live in their home, and these they assisted in their efforts to secure an education. These young people, now with families of their own, still sing the praises of this ideal home which they were permitted to share."[59]

Generativity, which is caring for and contributing to the next generation, is the term Erik Erikson used to describe the primary task of adulthood. Erickson further argued that "generative fathers" create, nurture, care for, and promote the development of other children, not merely their own.[60] David O. McKay seems to fit that term perfectly. Because of his ability to see beyond his own family and meet the needs of the next generation, he most certainly was a generative father.

Furthermore, a strong father keeps the promises and commitments he makes to his children. Not only would President David O.

McKay keep the commitments he made to his own children and grandchildren, he would do the same for other children as well. The prophet was a strong advocate of keeping promises. He believed that if you say something or make a promise, you must carry it out no matter what![61]

Consider the following example: As the President of the Church, he once promised two children that he would meet them in his office one morning at 7:00 a.m. Unfortunately, the day prior to the visit, Sister McKay became ill,[62] and President McKay would not leave her bedside. Clare Middlemiss, President McKay's secretary, was prepared to cancel the appointments. On the morning of the visits, however, President McKay called Clare and told her not to cancel the appointments, saying that he would not disappoint the children; he would keep his promise. His visit with the two youngsters and their parents was life changing.[63]

President McKay was consistent in the things that he taught and the way he conducted his life. As a father figure to not only his own children but to all children, David O. McKay demonstrated an unwavering commitment and loyalty to the next generation. He seemed to be able to balance Church work with family life, and the older he became, the more crystalized were his priorities.[64] Contemporary fathers would do well in following David O. McKay's example of being a committed father.

Many years ago, President McKay, in speaking to a group of Church employees, put into perspective where fathers' priorities should be. He said:

> Let me assure you, brethren, that someday you will have a Personal Priesthood Interview with the Savior Himself. If you are interested, I will tell you the order in which He will ask you to account for your earthly responsibilities.
>
> First, He will request an accountability report about your relationship with your wife. Have you actively been engaged in making her happy and ensuring that her needs have been met as an individual?

Second, He will want an accountability report about each of your children individually. He will not attempt to have this for simply a family stewardship report but will request information about your relationship to each and every child.

David O. McKay with two kids. (Courtesy of Intellectual Reserve, Inc.)

Third, He will want to know what you personally have done with the talents you were given in the pre-existence.

Fourth, He will want a summary of your activity in your Church assignments. He will not be necessarily interested in what assignments you have had, for in His eyes the home teacher and mission president are probably equals, but He will request a summary of how you have been of service to your fellowmen in your Church assignments.

Fifth, He will have no interest in how you earned your living, but if you were honest in all your dealings.

Sixth, He will ask for an accountability on what you have done to contribute in a positive manner to your community, state, country, and the world.[65]

Notice the emphasis on the relationships we have at home. For men, our priorities should be laser focused on our wives and children. Our actions should demonstrate our commitment. David O. McKay was an example of the rock-solid commitment that successful fathers must have in order to influence their children in positive ways that matter. David lived as he taught on this principle of commitment. There is little doubt that his family was his first priority and that he would rather be home than anywhere else. Although he traveled the world, he never felt complete without Emma Ray at his side and his children close by.

Notes

1. *Father, Consider Your Ways*, 4–5.

2. Paul Pearsall, *The Power of the Family* (New York: Bantam Books, 1991), 18.

3. M. Russell Ballard, "The Effects of Television," *Ensign*, May 1989, 19.

4. Kimberly Fisher and John Robinson, "Average Weekly Time Spent in 30 Basic Activities Across 17 Countries," *Social Indicators Research* 93, no. 1 (2009): 249–54.

5. William J. Bennett, *The Book of Man: Readings on the Path to Manhood* (Nashville: Thomas Nelson, 2011), xxii.

6. William J. Doherty and Barbara Carlson, *Putting Family First: Successful Strategies for Reclaiming Family Life in a Hurry-Up World* (New York: Henry Holt and Company, 2002), 101.

7. Doherty and Carlson, *Putting Family First*, 10.

8. Stephen R. Covey, *Seven Habits of Highly Effective Families* (New York: Golden Books, 1997), 113–14.

9. David C. Dollahite, Alan J. Hawkins, and Sean E. Brotherson, "Narrative Accounts, Generative Fathering, and Family Life Education," in *The Methods and Methodologies of Qualitative Family Research*, ed. Marvin B. Sussman and Jane F. Gilgun (New York: The Haworth Press, 1996), 356.

10. R. Koestner, C. Franz, and J. Weinberger, "The Family Origins of Empathic Concern: A 26-Year Longitudinal Study," *Journal of Personality and Social Psychology* 58, no. 4 (April 1990): 709–17.

11. As cited by Brent A. Barlow, "Marriage is Ordained of God," in *Brigham Young University 1999–2000 Speeches* (Brigham Young University Publications and Graphics, 2000), 51.

12. As cited in Gordon B. Hinckley, *Teachings of Gordon B. Hinckley* (Salt Lake City: Deseret Book, 1997), 201.

13. John Stewart, *Remembering the McKays* (Salt Lake City: Deseret Book, 1970), 24.

14. David O. McKay to Emma Ray McKay, 8 January 1907, David O. McKay Papers, MS 21606, box 1, folder 1, Church History Library, Salt Lake City. Hereafter, Church History Library will be cited as CHL.

15. David O. McKay to David L., Mildred, Llewelyn, Alice, Lou Jean, Russell, Emma Rae, Edward, and Robert, 25 October 1934, David O. McKay Papers, MS 668, box 1, folder 6, J. Willard Marriott Library, University of Utah, Salt Lake City. Hereafter, J. Willard Marriott Library, University of Utah, will be cited as Marriott Library.

16. Hereafter, David Lawrence McKay will be referred to as Lawrence in body text and David L. McKay in endnotes.

17. Mary Jane Woodger, *David O. McKay: Beloved Prophet* (American Fork, UT: Covenant Communications, 2004), 72.

18. J. E. McCullough, *Home: The Savior of Civilization* (Southern co-operative league, 1924), 42, quoted in Ezra Taft Benson, in Conference Report, April 1935, 116.

19. President Ezra Taft Benson taught, "Fathers, yours is an eternal calling from which you are never released. Callings in the Church, as important as they are, by their very nature are only for a period of time, and then an appropriate release takes place. But a father's calling is eternal, and its importance transcends time. It is a calling for both time and eternity." Ezra Taft Benson, "To the Fathers of Israel," *Ensign*, November 1987, 48–50.

20. Harold B. Lee, address to Seminary and Institute personnel at Brigham Young University Summer School, 8 July 1966; see also Harold B. Lee, *Decisions for Successful Living* (Salt Lake City: Deseret Book, 1973), 248–49.

21. Francis Gibbons wrote that "their mutual love of music, good books, and beautiful decor gave assurance that their home would be one of culture and refinement. And their shared convictions about the divinity of the restored Church and their faith in God introduced a spiritual quality into the home that manifested itself in regular family and personal prayers and in love, kindness, and forgiveness." Francis Gibbons, *David O. McKay: Apostle to the World, Prophet of God* (Salt Lake City: Deseret Book, 1986), 61–62.

22. Woodger, *David O. McKay*, 91.

23. McKay Microfilm, 19 March 1907, reel 3:429, CHL.

24. Diaries of David O. McKay, April 1906 to June 1907, MS 668, box 4, folder 1, Marriott Library, 78–80.

25. Gibbons, *David O. McKay*, 75.

26. David L. McKay, microfilm, address at a Luncheon of the 17th Annual Meeting of the Mormon History Association, 8 May 1982, MS 7013, CHL.

27. Jeanette McKay Morrell, "Life of President David O. McKay: A Few Highlights of a Busy Life," *Relief Society Magazine*, November 1953, 733.

28. David O. McKay to Emma Ray McKay, 8 June 1907, David O. McKay Family Papers, 1897–1954, MS 21606, box 1, folder 1, CHL.

29. David O. McKay to Emma Ray McKay, 14 June 1906, David O. McKay Papers, MS 668, box 1, folder 3, Marriott Library.

30. David O. McKay to Emma Ray McKay, 8 December 1910, David O. McKay Papers, MS 668, box 1, folder 3, Marriott Library.

31. David L. McKay, "Remembering Father and Mother, President David O. McKay and Sister Emma Ray Riggs McKay," *Ensign*, August 1984, 34–36.

32. David O. McKay, *Gospel Ideals: Selections from the Discourses of David O. McKay* (Salt Lake City: Deseret Book, 1953), 455.

33. David O. McKay to Emma Ray McKay, 8 December 1910, David O. McKay Papers, MS 668, box 1, folder 3, Marriott Library.

34. David O. McKay to Emma Ray McKay, 15 June 1907, David O. McKay Family Papers, 1897–1954, MS 21606, box 1, folder 1, CHL.

35. David O. McKay to Emma Ray McKay, 11 June 1907, David O. McKay Family Papers, 1897–1954, MS 21606, box 1, folder 1, CHL.

36. David O. McKay to Emma Ray McKay, 8 June 1907, David O. McKay Family Papers, 1897–1954, MS 21606, box 1, folder 1, CHL.

37. David O. McKay to Emma Ray McKay, 27 July 1907, David O. McKay Family Papers, 1897–1954, MS 21606, box 1, folder 1, CHL.

38. Diaries of David O. McKay, April 1906 to June 1907, MS 668, box 4, folder 1, Marriott Library, 85.

39. David O. McKay to Emma Ray McKay, 13 March 1909, David O. McKay Family Papers, 1897–1954, MS 21606, box 1, folder 1, CHL.

40. David O. McKay to Emma Ray McKay, 20 May 1909, David O. McKay Family Papers, 1897–1954, MS 21606, box 1, folder 1, CHL.

41. Diaries of David O. McKay, April 1906 to June 1907, MS 668, box 4, folder 2, Marriott Library, 78–80.

42. Diaries of David O. McKay, March 1908 to March 1909, MS 668, box 4, folder 3, Marriott Library, 78–80, 63.

43. Diaries of David O. McKay, April 1906 to June 1907, MS 668, box 4, folder 2, Marriott Library, 78–81.

44. Diaries of David O. McKay, March 1908 to March 1909, MS 668, box 4, folder 3, Marriott Library, 78–80, 139.

45. Diaries of David O. McKay, March 1908 to March 1909, MS 668, box 4, folder 3, Marriott Library, 157–58.

46. Diaries of David O. McKay, December 1920, MS 668, box 6, folder 11, Marriott Library; emphasis in original.

47. Diaries of David O. McKay, December 1920, MS 668, box 6, folder 11, Marriott Library; emphasis in original.

48. Diaries of David O. McKay, January to February 1921, MS 668, box 6, folder 14, Marriott Library; emphasis in original.

49. Shortly after boarding the ship for his world tour with Hugh J. Cannon, David sat down and began writing letters to his family, who he already missed. He wrote: "Before and after dinner, I spent every moment in the reading room writing letters to friends and Loved ones at home. When the moment came to leave dear old America—even Canadian America, there were some pretty lonesome feelings tugging away at my heart-strings. . . . Up to the moment of boarding the ship, I seemed to be imbued with the feeling that I usually have when attending a quarterly conference—at the conclusion of which I would board the train and return to home and loved ones; but when the boat begins to move . . . thousands of thousands and tens of thousands of miles of ocean travel lay between home and me, I feel downright gloomy." Diaries of David O. McKay, March 1908 to March 1909, MS 668, box 6, folder 14, Marriott Library.

50. David O. McKay to Emma Ray McKay, D.O., 7 June 1929, David O. McKay Papers, MS 668, box 4, folder 3, Marriott Library; emphasis in original.

51. Diaries of David O. McKay, February to April 1921, MS 668, box 6, folder 15, Marriott Library.

52. After the first part of the world tour was completed, David and Hugh Cannon met their families in San Francisco. It was the first time David had seen Emma Ray and the children for months. It was a quick meeting before their boat left port again. He wrote in his diary: "If only life could be made up of happy meetings, and there were no partings. [What a blessing] life would be! After all, this is just what our concept of heaven is. Parting from my Sweetheart and dear kiddies was quite as difficult this morning as if it was Dec. 4, 1920!" Diaries of David O. McKay, February to April 1921, MS 668, box 6, folder 4, Marriott Library.

53. As cited by J. Ballard Washburn, "The Temple is a Family Affair," *Ensign*, May 1995, 12.

54. Llewelyn R. McKay, *Home Memories of President David O. McKay* (Salt Lake City: Deseret Book, 1956), 139–41.

55. President David O. McKay taught that "men today in far too great an extent are . . . spending their time with things which have no permanent value," in Conference Report, October 1942, 67. As a father, David understood this concept, and, undoubtedly, so did his children. They were the beneficiaries of his belief that children have permanent, lasting, and eternal value.

56. Once, when traveling as an Apostle to southern Utah, David had dinner at the home of Brigham Young Jr.'s widow, who was living in the San Juan Stake at the time. David wrote in his diary, "After dinner played ball with her boy Walter and some of his companions." Diaries of David O. McKay, April 1906 to June 1907, MS 668, box 4, folder 2, Marriott Library. For this Apostle of the Lord, playing ball with a fatherless son was not beneath his dignity. In fact, he may have even felt some responsibility and even privileged to play ball with Brigham Young's grandson.

57. Llewelyn R. McKay, *Home Memories of President David O. McKay*, 136–37.

58. Ibid.

59. Morrell, "Life of President David O. McKay," 47.

60. John Snarey, "The Next Generation of Work on Fathering," in *Generative Fathering*, ed. David C. Dollahite and Alan J. Hawkins (Thousand Oaks, CA: Sage, 1997), ix.

61. David Lawrence McKay, *My Father, David O. McKay* (Salt Lake City: Deseret Book, 1989), 99.

62. In the newspaper, a notice appeared that Sister McKay had been seriously injured. Morrell, "Life of President David O. McKay," 285.

63. Morrell, "Life of President David O. McKay," 285–86.

64. Historian Francis Gibbons observed, "At an early age he was disciplined to the juggler's art—the skill of keeping many balls in the air at once without allowing any of them to fall to the ground. It required a deft touch, supreme concentration of effort, and adroit maneuvering so that nothing was left unattended despite the strict economy of time imposed on any one activity." Gibbons, *David O. McKay*, 76.

65. This statement was given in June 1965; from the notes of Fred A. Baker, a managing director of the Church's Department of Physical Facilities, as cited in Alexander B. Morrison, *Feed My Sheep* (Salt Lake City: Deseret Book, 1992), 156.

3

Creative Father

"There is no home without love. You may have a palace and yet not have a home,
and you may live in a log house with a dirt roof, and a dirt floor, and have there
the most glorious home in all the world, if within those four log walls there
permeates the divine principle of love."
—David O. McKay[1]

Home sweet home! How good it always is to return home after being gone for some time. College students long to return home for Christmas after a lengthy and busy semester at college. Those in the military long for the day they can return home and embrace their families. Likewise, missionaries anticipate the day they can return home and rejoice with their loved ones. Truly, there is no place like home. The home is the place where wise parents teach their children "faith, prayer, repentance, forgiveness, respect, love, compassion, work, and wholesome recreational activities."[2] Home is a refuge from the storms of life; home is the laboratory of love. The late Elder Marvin J. Ashton of the Quorum of the Twelve Apostles added that home should be "where life's greatest lessons are taught and learned. Home can be the center of one's earthly faith where love and mutual responsibility are blended."[3]

Dollahite, Hawkins, and Brotherson have suggested that creativity is an attribute that strong fathers possess. However, creativity, in this case, does not imply that successful fathers merely conjure up or fabricate activities and experiences for their children to participate in. Dollahite, Hawkins, and Brotherson have explained that "the responsibility and capability to create involve the call and capacity to meet a child's needs through work that produces or procures resources and opportunities for the child."[4]

Creating, then, suggests that successful fathers (1) provide for their families, (2) use their resources to create opportunities for their children, and (3) fashion an environment where their children can be successful. Such fathers are intentional and deliberate regarding their "creative" works and efforts. Moreover, such fathers help their children solve problems, and create opportunities for the growth and development of their families.

Strong fathers are men who create an atmosphere, provide opportunities, construct activities for growth and happiness, and forge an environment where their children can flourish. Therefore, creative fathering could include moving to a safe and healthy neighborhood, implementing a new and innovative idea for a family party, providing the material resources for piano lessons or a club team, or giving children opportunities to succeed in school.

Fathers can also help create an environment at home that is conducive to helping children feel safe and secure. Sometimes, fathers dream that they must provide a home for their children with tennis courts, swimming pools, and horses in order for their children to have idyllic childhoods. Yet disciples of Christ need not be reared at country clubs with a tennis racquet in one hand and cotton candy in the other. A spiritual environment in the home is what Latter-day Saint children need.[5] President McKay recommended that parents create a home environment with proper literature, music, and artwork. He also urged parents to teach their children to sing.[6] He further stated, "I know of no other place than home where more happiness can be found in this life. It is possible to make home a bit of heaven; indeed, I picture heaven to be a continuation of the ideal home."[7]

There are simple things fathers can do in order to provide a healthy environment at home. Ronald Molen suggests that every home should have the following:

1. *A place to gather* where people can sit and chat comfortably. Maybe around a fireplace or a conversation pit. A place where family members naturally gather in order to relax and visit.

2. *A place to dine*—not just a bar where people grab their microwave dinners, but a place where the family can sit together for dinner and talk. Eating on the run or in front of the television leaves family members leading separate lives. Eating together can be a great time for sharing.

3. *A place to play and relax*. Children need a place where they can finger paint or create things with Playdough without getting into trouble. Children need a place where playing and creating is encouraged. Maybe there are murals or ladders, ropes, platforms, a fireman's pole. It can be a place that is colorful and fun. . . .

4. *A place to be alone*. Maybe it is a bedroom or quiet room where a child can read, think, study, build a model airplane, or do whatever else they want.

5. *A place to remember* might be an attic room, a dormer window, or a treehouse. A place for reading mysteries or adventure stories. A magical place that children will remember.[8]

Additionally, President McKay suggested there are a couple of other necessary ingredients for a proper home environment. He taught, "A child has the right to feel that in his home he has a place of refuge, a place of protection from the dangers and evils of the outside world."[9]

David O. McKay was successful in providing such an environment for his children. The McKays were not a wealthy family. In fact, for most of their lives, they struggled financially. Many of David's letters to Emma Ray are filled with discussions on juggling finances to make ends meet.[10] However, they provided everything for their children that money could not buy.[11] Their home environment was conducive to the spiritual development, intellectual development, and emotional development of their children.[12]

Creating a Spiritual Environment in the Home

President David O. McKay declared, "A true Mormon home is one in which if Christ should chance to enter, he would be pleased to linger and to rest."[13] Furthermore, he urged parents to "make accessible to children proper literature, music, and appropriate motion pictures."[14] David was concerned that many Latter-day Saint homes were not holding the interest of children; consequently, they were going into deviant places to be entertained. He taught, "Our homes should be more attractive and . . . more of our amusements should be in the home instead of out on the streets."[15]

One way that David O. McKay demonstrated his creativity as a father was by reading and telling stories to his children. He would also take his children to see plays and other dramatic events.[16] His daughter Lou Jean recounted vivid memories of sitting on her father's lap while he read the children "The Lady of the Lake," *Ivanhoe*, and *The Blue Bird*. David Lawrence remembered:

> [David O. McKay's] diary for 24 February 1914 records: "With David Lawrence, Llewelyn and Lou Jean, I . . . went to the Theatre to see 'The Blue Bird,' a most beautiful drama by Maeterlink. Children enjoy the scenery and the children actors; the grown people, the philosophy." *The Lady of the Lake* was a family favorite, sometimes continued over several tellings. We loved the poetry and the Scots dialect in which Father told the story. It's hard for me to separate his telling it from the books that we later discovered on our own. I recall reading Walter Scott's *Marmion* but without much enthusiasm because Father had never told us that story."[17]

Creating Fun and Making Memories

There were other ways President McKay "created" for his children and his grandchildren. One of his favorite activities was sleigh riding. Even into his eighties, he took the children and grandchildren on sleigh rides during every Christmas vacation. Lawrence related how fun it was to see his father driving the children and grandchildren, wearing "his long thick raccoon coat and big gloves, beaming from ear to ear."[18] When David's brother Thomas was serving as a mission president in Europe, David wrote to him on 17 February 1939, "Did anyone tell you about the sleigh ride we had with our grandchildren,

David O. McKay sleigh riding with his kids and grandkids. (Courtesy of Intellectual Reserve, Inc.)

including their parents, Lawrence, Mildred, and Llewellyn? We had a glorious time—the joys of our youth were with us again!"[19] It must have meant a lot to David for him to even mention this experience in a letter. During the warmer months, David was also instrumental in organizing games of baseball and croquet on the lawn in Huntsville with his children and grandchildren.[20] As the President of the Church, he taught: "Every period of human life is wonderful; the irresponsible age of childhood, the thrilling years of adolescence and courtship, the productive, fighting, burden-bearing era of parenthood; but the most wonderful time of life comes when the father and mother become chums of their grown-up, successful sons and daughters, and can begin to enjoy their children's children."[21]

Indeed, President and Sister McKay had become great friends with their own children and took great pride and joy in their posterity. Being with his family was a source of great strength and rejuvenation for this busy Church leader.

Creating Poetry

Creating, of course, is not only limited to creating a healthy home environment. Strong fathers also seem to have the ability to think "outside the box" and are willing to take chances and construct activities and experiences that require that the greatest creative juices be flowing. They are the king of fathers who create a campground in the family living room, complete with tents and sleeping bags, or they take their children to the airport just to watch planes takeoff or land.

In that spirit, another aspect of creativity in the life of President McKay was the poetry he wrote for his children. When his daughter Emma Rae moved out of the home and took a teaching job in McCammon, Idaho, David missed her so much. He wrote her:

> Lonesome seems the home today, yet four of us are here!
> The sun is shining brightly, yet there's an absence, sure, of cheer!
> Mother—tearful—still is smiling, and the boys pretend to play,
> But home is not the same—now that Emma's gone away![22]

On another occasion, David "repurchased" a violin for his son Lawrence. Lawrence had sold the violin to attend law school. David and Emma Ray bought the violin back and returned it to Lawrence, along with the following poem:

> This viol I know isn't the best of its kind,
> But it's won a place in my heart and mind
> Which no Stradivarius can fill.
> So I've bought it again for connoted joy,
> And the tones it gave forth at the touch of our boy—
> I recall them e'en now with a thrill.[23]

This was the same violin that Lawrence played in his family's three-piece orchestra, where Llewelyn played the clarinet, and Lou Jean played the piano. The children frequently performed at family nights and on other occasions. Lou Jean related, "One of father's joys was to sit (sometimes for hours) and listen to the trio. . . . It seemed to relax him to listen to strains from II Trovatore, Schubert's Barcarole, Angel's Serenade or the sextet from Lucia."[24]

Creative Work Opportunities

Furthermore, David O. McKay's beloved Huntsville and Dry Hollow Farm always provided creative opportunities for him to teach his children to work and to be responsible. Every chance David had, he took one or more of his children and headed up the windy canyon road to Huntsville. In the summers, the family would move from Ogden to the farm. By doing so, David did his best to ensure that his sons would learn excellent work habits. Many of David's diary entries record visits to the family farm and being with his children.

After Lawrence, Llewelyn, and Lou Jean left home, David and Emma Ray were still left with Emma Rae, Edward, and Robert. Because of David's duties in the Quorum of the Twelve, it was finally time to leave Ogden and move to a large apartment in Salt Lake City. Nevertheless, at the age of fifty-one, President McKay still maintained the farm in Huntsville to teach his sons Ned (Edward) and Bobby (Robert) how to work.[25] Even in his sixties, when most men would be facing retirement, David was working the farm and teaching his young sons to work. His 1935 and 1936 diaries record the following:

> Saturday, May 4th, 1935, 'Office during the forenoon—Huntsville in the afternoon. Ned and Bobby accompanied me.'

> Thursday, July 11th, 1935, '4:00 a.m. on the farm raking hay with Ned and Bobby. [The diary reports that by 8:30 he was heading to Salt Lake City, and by 10:00 a.m. he was in a council meeting.']

> Saturday, October 19th, 1935, 'In Huntsville with Ned, Bobby, and others digging potatoes on Dry Hollow Farm.'[26]

> Saturday, April 11th, 1936, 'Bobbie and I drove to Ogden and Huntsville in the afternoon.'

> Saturday, May 16th, 1936, 'Office duties in the forenoon. At 12 noon, Ned, Bobby, and I drove to Huntsville, and assisted Dale Newey in finishing preparation of five acres of land for peas.'

> Saturday, May 23rd, 1936, 1:00 p.m., 'Bobby and I drove to Huntsville, and spent two or three hours working in Dry Hollow.'[27]

One of President McKay's beliefs was that the "real test of any Church or religion is the kind of men it makes."[28] Aside from the teachings of the gospel, David was convinced that teaching his sons to work hard would make them into hardworking and responsible men, fathers, and priesthood leaders. Many of his diaries are silent most of the year

David O. McKay with a favorite horse.
(Courtesy of Intellectual Reserve, Inc.)

except for the occasions where he worked on the farm with his boys. They drove cattle,[29] worked with hogs,[30] shoveled snow, cut hay,[31] plowed ditches,[32] and planted trees, shrubs, potatoes, and peas.[33] His formula seems to have worked, as each of his sons attained marks of success in their home lives, in Church service, and on a professional level. It seemed that President McKay was the happiest when he was working with his family on the farm in Huntsville.

Creating a Home for Grandchildren

Strong fathers and grandfathers are typically willing to create an environment that is conducive to build family memories and family fun. Many contemporary grandparents move into apartments, assisted-living centers, and even condominiums. One of the significant perks to such downsizing is zero yardwork and considerably less upkeep on the homestead. However, such dwellings are not always "kid friendly," with little room to roam and few things to do. David O. McKay and Emma Ray came up with a solution to that problem.

After living in a Salt Lake City apartment for many years, they decided to purchase a home in Salt Lake City. It was a two-story red-brick home on South Temple Street. The home had a yard "where exuberant grandchildren could exhaust their pent-up energies and yet be near enough for grand-parental supervision—and enjoyment."[34]

Here we see a family patriarch creating an environment in his home so that all could laugh and have an enjoyable time.[35] He was willing to create spiritual, intellectual, entertainment, and athletic opportunities for his family. As a result, these legacies were passed through the generations. They continue to keep the McKay family bonded together today.

David O. McKay and grandkids around a piano. (Courtesy of Intellectual Reserve, Inc.)

President McKay understood that family was his most important priority. Although he was busy, he made sure that he created memories, created opportunities, and strengthened relationships while he was with his family. In that vein, Elder Dallin H. Oaks shared an experience. While he was the president of Brigham Young University, he had a weekly coordination meeting with Neal A. Maxwell, the Church commissioner of education. Elder Oaks related that in one particular meeting, Neal Maxwell began by asking, "What should you like to be remembered for after you are released from your present positions?" Brother Maxwell then asked each person in the meeting to write their answer on a piece of paper and ponder it. As President Oaks contemplated that question, his mind traveled from Brigham Young University to his home. As a father, he asked himself, "When your children are grown up and leave home, or when you die, what do you want them to remember about you as a father?" Elder Oaks reported, "This question caused me to see that I was in danger of being remembered for always being critical and nagging about trivial behaviors that irritated me, such as the practice of a teenage daughter who continually scattered her clothes and other possessions all around the house. I wanted to be remembered for fatherly communications of praise and love and other matters of eternal importance. Those are the communications whose memories have persuasive power."[36]

David O. McKay understood what he would be remembered for as a husband, father, and grandfather. If there is one thing David O. McKay created more than anything else, it was family memories. He constantly worked on creating an environment in his home where his family and the Savior could dwell. He also built a situation in Huntsville where his family could connect by working and playing together. These creative environments provided havens of spiritual peace and happiness.

Notes

1. David O. McKay, in Conference Report, June 1919, 78.

2. The First Presidency and Council of the Twelve Apostles, "The Family: A Proclamation to the World," *Ensign*, November 2010, 129.

3. Marvin J. Ashton, *Ye Are My Friends* (Salt Lake City: Deseret Book, 1982), 44.

4. David C. Dollahite, Alan J. Hawkins, and Sean E. Brotherson, "Fatherwork: A Conceptual Ethic of Fathering as Generative Work," in *Generative Fathering: Beyond Deficit Perspectives*, ed. Alan J. Hawkins and David C. Dollahite (Thousand Oaks, CA: Sage, 1997), 31.

5. President McKay taught in a general conference, "Let us go back to our homes and see whether the spirit of our homes is such that if an angel called, he would be pleased to remain." David O. McKay, in Conference Report, October 1951, 161.

6. David O. McKay, *Pathways to Happiness* (Salt Lake City: Deseret Book, 1957), 121.

7. David O. McKay, *Gospel Ideals*, 490.

8. Ronald L. Molen, *House, Plus Environment* (Salt Lake City: Olympus Publishing, 1974), 41–46, emphasis in original; as cited in H. Wallace Goddard, *The Frightful and Joyous Journey of Family Life: Applying Gospel Insights in the Home* (Salt Lake City: Bookcraft, 1997), 116–17.

9. David O. McKay, in Conference Report, April 1945, 144.

10. Diaries of David O. McKay, April 1906 to June 1907, MS 668, box 4, folder 1, Marriott Library.

11. President McKay taught parents that the great need in American homes is more religion. He further explained, "Parents should make it obvious both by their actions and their conversation that they are seriously interested . . . in the fruits of true religion." He also emphasized that discussing religion in the home should be as natural as employees in offices talking about golf, parties, and profits. See David O. McKay, in Conference Report, October 1946, 115.

12. President McKay taught that all children are entitled to three things: (1) a respected name, (2) a sense of security, and (3) opportunities for development. See David O. McKay, in Conference Report, April 1935, 113.

13. David O. McKay, in Conference Report, October 1947, 120.

14. David O. McKay, "The Greatest Trust, the Greatest Joy," *Instructor*, April 1964, 253.

15. David O. McKay, *Gospel Ideals*, 485–86.

16. His children were extremely familiar with Shakespeare. See Woodger, *David O. McKay*, 94.

17. McKay, *My Father, David O. McKay*, 89.

18. McKay, *My Father, David O. McKay*, 70.

19. Thomas E. McKay Papers, MSS 1442, Letters Sent and Received by Thomas E. McKay and His Brother, David O. McKay, box 1, folder 3, L. Tom Perry Special Collections, Harold B. Lee Library, Brigham Young University, Provo, UT. Hereafter, any sources from the L. Tom Perry Special Collections will be cited as LTPSC, Lee Library.

20. Horseback riding was another way he connected with his children and grandchildren. David L. McKay, interview by Gordon Irving, The James Moyle Oral History Program, Salt Lake City, January–May 1984, MS 200 734, 132, CHL.

21. David O. McKay, in Conference Report, April 1953, 16–17.

22. Llewelyn McKay, *Home Memories of President David O. McKay*, 174–75.

23. Llewelyn McKay, *Home Memories of President David O. McKay*, 179.

24. Francis Gibbons, *David O. McKay*, 63.

25. Keith Terry, *David O. McKay: Prophet of Love* (Santa Barbara, CA: Butterfly Publishing, 1980), 95.

26. Diaries of David O. McKay, January to December 1935, MS 668, box 7, folder 13, Marriott Library,

27. Diaries of David O. McKay, January to October 1936, MS 668, box 7, folder 14, Marriott Library,

28. David O. McKay, in Conference Report, April 1949, 11.

29. Diaries of David O. McKay, February to December 1912, MS 668, box 5, folder 2, Marriott Library.

30. Diaries of David O. McKay, August to December 1915, MS 668, box 5, folder 4, Marriott Library.

31. Diaries of David O. McKay, January to December 1932, MS 668, box 7, folder 11, Marriott Library.

32. Diaries of David O. McKay, January to December 1937, MS 668, box 8, folder 2, Marriott Library.

33. Diaries of David O. McKay, January to December 1932, MS 668, box 7, folder 11, Marriott Library.

34. Francis Gibbons, *David O. McKay*, 188.

35. David and Emma Ray were also excellent grandparents. In their Salt Lake City home, they had the grandchildren over quite often. For Christmas dinner, the adults usually sat around the large kitchen table while the children ate their meals on several card tables. At one Christmas dinner, the adults were laughing and carrying on while the grandchildren, sitting at their card tables, wondered what all the fuss was about. One granddaughter basically said, "What were you laughing about? We couldn't hear it." Immediately, President David O. McKay changed the family tradition on the spot. He said, "Christmas is for the children." From that point on, the grandchildren sat at the large table, and the adults sat at the card tables, which they moved closer to the main table. Because of this, everyone could laugh together! See David L. McKay, interview by Gordon Irving, James Moyle Oral History Program, Salt Lake City, January–May 1984, MS 200 734, 132, CHL.

36. Dallin H. Oaks, *Life's Lessons Learned* (Salt Lake City: Deseret Book, 2011), 61–62.

4

Nurturing Father

"You are not going to bring back erring youth unless you first let them know
that you are interested in them. Let them feel your heart touch. Only the
warm heart can kindle warmth in another.... The kind hand or the loving
arm removes suspicion and awakens confidence."
—David O. McKay[1]

To be a nurturing father is to be a father who cares about his children, who is involved in their lives, and who encourages their development and growth. Nurturing fathers must have a positive, healthy relationship with each of their children. Without such a relationship, fathers will have little influence on their children.[2]

Elder Robert D. Hales stated, "In many ways earthly parents represent their Heavenly Father in the process of nurturing, loving, caring [for], and teaching children. Children naturally look to their parents to learn of the characteristics of their Heavenly Father. After they come to love, respect, and have confidence in their earthly parents, they often unknowingly develop the same feelings towards their Heavenly Father."[3] It was Brigham Young who encouraged fathers to treat their families "as an angel would treat them."[4]

As fathers strive to be Christlike, they will hopefully desire to treat their children in a manner that the Savior would treat them. Nurturing fathers should not only demonstrate care and concern for their children but also should attempt to recognize the needs of their children and then attempt to meet those needs. Strong fathers should provide for their children what they need at the time they most need it.[5] Nurturing fathers continually strive to be actively involved in their children's lives. Simply put, these men are involved with their kids. Such men are not afraid to show affection towards their children. David O. McKay was this kind of father. He demonstrated care and concern as he waited upon his children and showed them affection. And, for a busy man, he was involved in their lives.

Tuned In

President David O. McKay taught, "Parents cannot with impunity shirk the responsibility to protect childhood and youth."[6] Even though David was gone much of the time, his family was constantly on his mind. For example, on Wednesday, 31 July 1907, he wrote in his diary from Denver: "I am worried as I write this because I feel that all is not well at home. . . . Sent a telegram to Ray inquiring about the children."[7] It seemed that throughout his travels, the Spirit prompted him to know when his children were sick or otherwise afflicted.

Much of David O. McKay's care, concern, and desire to protect are evident in the letters he wrote to his family while he was away on Church business. For example, shortly after his call to the Quorum of the Twelve, he wrote Emma Ray from Cedar City, Utah:

> Had a pleasant rest last night, and feel well this morning. I dreamed, however, that Lawrence nearly got run over by an automobile. The little hero kept his head and schemed to escape. It seemed so real, I feel a little worried. Don't stay alone nights. Get Annie and Tom to occupy the little room. I wish I could give you a Birthday kiss, but I must keep it and give it with interest when we meet. Kiss baby and Lawrence. Accept my truest love, and believe me.
>
> Your own, Dade[8]

From this letter, it is easy to detect that Emma Ray and the children occupied his mind constantly. Here he was, on a stake conference assignment, worried about Lawrence and dreaming of a potential accident. This dream prompted David to ask Emma Ray not to stay alone at night.

Sickness, Loss, and Grief

One of the challenges that both David and Emma Ray had to contend with was dealing with sick children. Like other parents in the early 1900s, the McKays had children that were stricken with coughs, colds, pneumonia, measles, flu, and a host of other illnesses. It was difficult for Emma Ray to shoulder the load of tending to her sick children while balancing her many other responsibilities. At the same time, it broke David's heart to leave his worn-out wife and sick children behind as he traveled the world as an Apostle. The most acute anxiety he faced was worrying for his wife and sick children. For example, on Friday, 2 August 1907, he was relieved because he had just returned from a stake conference assignment, and the children were sick. He wrote in his diary that when he arrived home, the baby "was very sick, she had been for two weeks. Lawrence was better; Llewelyn, ailing. . . . Spent a happy day with Ray and our babies."[9]

On Tuesday, 13 August, David reported that he arrived home at 6:45 a.m. to find their baby still very sick: "Lawrence with a severe cold in addition to his cough, and Ray quite worn out."[10] During the month of October 1907, sickness continued in the McKay home. David recorded that on Friday, 25 October 1907, his little daughter had contracted pneumonia, "and today we are anxious about her condition. Her fever is high . . . spent a night of anxiety."[11] On Sunday, 27 October 1907, David wrote that his daughter was still sick but that her health was improving. However, he stayed home for the entire next week helping Emma Ray and the babies.[12]

Perhaps one of the most tender and sacred experiences for David as a father occurred when their young son, Royle, became very sick. Initially, the baby seemed to have pain in his knee, accompanied by fever and lethargy. Royle was diagnosed with rheumatism. Meanwhile, it was the April general conference, and David had church responsibilities to tend to. He wrote in his diary: "Learning by telephone that baby is worse, I returned home at 11:45 p.m. Poor little Royle! He is suffering from an infected knee, probably caused by a fall. The doctors do not know what is the matter; but Dr. Morrell thinks the infection has been in his system since his recent illness. Baby seems a little better, but his fever is still around 104."[13]

David must have gone back to the conference the next morning. He wrote in his diary that he was present at the Salt Lake Tabernacle at 10:00 a.m. Immediately after the morning session of the conference, the following occurred: "At noon, I learned by telegram that Royle will probably have to be taken to the hospital. [I] feel that I ought to miss the afternoon meeting and go home to my wife and baby boy, but finally concluded to remain until 4:00 p.m. . . . . Up all night with our sick boy. Fever has been 106."[14]

The following day, 7 April 1912, David wrote that at 3:30 a.m., Royle had two seizures within a two-hour time period. He further recorded:

> The Doctors have concluded that his only hope is in having an operation, and this is extremely hazardous because of the congenital weakness in his heart.
>
> The operation was performed under the direction of three doctors . . . Dr. Morrell supervising. Everything was successful. The diagnosis had been just right. At 10:35 a.m. all was over, and we felt encouraged.
>
> He soon recovered from the effects of the anesthetic, and was less feverish and entirely conscious all day, but towards the night his breathing became short, and his fever began to rise.
>
> He was evidently in great pain from some other cause besides his little afflicted leg. O what a night of suffering for our darling boy! Every breath he drew seemed agony to him!
>
> The doctors examined him this morning and discovered that his pain was due to Pleurisy on both sides. At this, we almost lost hope, but later when Dr. Morrell told us that by an examination he

knew what germ had caused the infection, and that he had the anti-toxin, we again took courage.

But Royle was too weak, and complications of diseases too many. He battled bravely all day, taking the little stimulant given him at intervals as willingly as a grown person would. About 9:30 p.m. Papa, Thomas E., and I again administered to him. Ray felt very hopeful, and lay down. . . . beside him for a little rest.

Soon his little pulse weakened, and we knew that our baby would soon leave us. "Mama" was the last word on his . . . lips. Just before the end came, he stretched out his little hands, and as I stooped to caress him, he encircled my neck, and gave me the last of many of the most loving caresses ever a father received from a darling child. It seemed he realized he was going, and wanted to say, "Good-bye papa," but his little voice was already stilled by weakness and pain. . . . Death had taken our baby boy.

The end came at 1:50 a.m. without even a twitch of a muscle. "He is not dead but sleepeth" was never more applicable to any soul, for he truly went to sleep—He did not die.[15]

To read this account is heart-wrenching. The days following Royle's passing were somber in the McKay home. It took the family more than a short while to get their "legs under them again." In the years that followed, Royle was often on the mind of David and Emma Ray. Each Memorial Day that followed his death, the family stopped by the Ogden Cemetery to pay tribute to Royle.[16]

Dealing with Homesickness

One of the most difficult journeys for David was the world tour of 1920–21. With traveling companion Hugh J. Cannon, David went from one end of the earth to the other. There were times of danger, and of course there were many spiritual experiences. The most diffi-cult aspect of the entire experience for David was being away from his family for such an extended period of time. On this voyage, David's letters to Emma Ray and the children were rich and deep.

David O. McKay with Tongan kids. (Courtesy of Intellectual Reserve, Inc.)

For example, he wrote:

> I'm really homesick this morning. This monotonous life in the month of June is beginning to tell on my nerves. Last night and this morning I've thought almost continuously about the folks at home. . . . I can even now see the kiddies playing on the lawn, Mama and Lou Jean on the summer porch, and Llewelyn on his way to the Dry Hollow farm. June 11th I imagined him coming home with feet soaked and trousers wet to the hips, but happy because he caught four fish. . . . If I were home, I should be in a better place, but Travelers must be content.[17]

On 5 May 1921, after being away from home a short five months (relative to the entire trip), he wrote his daughter Lou Jean, while aboard the SS *Tofua*:

> My darling Lou Jean:
>
>   If you knew with what tenderness I have written "My darling Lou Jean," this morning, you would have an absolute assurance that

whatever else may come to you in life, you have a father who loves you dearly.

If this world tour does nothing else, it will imprint upon my soul everlastingly how dearly I love your sweet mother and you children! I've often said to mama that I did not believe that "absence makes the heart grow fonder," nor do I this morning. If that were true the world would die of grief for loved ones gone. I do believe, however, that a little absence does increase one's fondness.[18]

While on the same ship, David received a telegram from Emma Ray, indicating that all was well at home, and that she missed him very much. David wrote back, "As this was the first line from home since I left March 26th,[19] you don't blame me for shedding a tear or two. Everybody well, and hearts still warm! What else matters? Health and Love are after all the greatest blessings of life. With these as our assets, we shall one day be out of debt; and, in the meantime by happy as cooing doves."[20]

Father Kind and Dear

David O. McKay taught in general conference, "Homes are made permanent through love. Oh, then, let love abound. If you feel that you have not the love of those little boys and girls, study to get it. Though you neglect some of the cattle, though you fail to produce good crops, even, study to hold your children's love."[21]

David deeply loved his children and expressed that love through his words and deeds. For example, he brought Lawrence with him on a Church trip to Kanab, Utah. While there, the weather took an extreme turn for the worse, and flash floods encompassed the area. David wrote to Emma the next day, "My anxiety for Lawrence was worse than the dreariness of the night. But we were blessed and protected. We passed through perilous places that day, and escaped without one serious mishap."[22] It is easy to detect David's deep feelings and concern for his son. It must have been a harrowing experience for him to even mention it.

Years later, Lawrence provided more details of this experience. He related that as soon as they got off the train in Marysvale, they were met

David O. McKay enjoyed riding.

by the stake president, Joseph Houston, and the weather was treacherous. They traveled the fifty miles to Panguitch in a buggy, getting drenched in the deluge. The next day, they traveled another thirty miles in their buggy to Cannonville to set apart a new bishop. David reported, "I remember watching the red mud coming up and falling off the wheels all day." Eventually, the party came to a river that they decided to cross. The water was up to the horses' bellies. They drove for a while along the side of the mountains, but there were big rocks coming down. They turned back, but by now, the river had risen, and the water was moving swiftly. They had no way to cross, and they were trapped.

Lawrence said, "I thought it was the end of the world and I started to cry. Father took me in his arms and held me all night, keeping me dry. Finally, I went to sleep. In the morning, the flood had subsided and two men came on horseback across what was left of it and guided us to Cannonville."[23]

Lawrence concluded from that experience, "It's hard to disobey a man who loves you and puts his arms around you."[24] The love between father and son here is obvious. Here is a good example of a father, willing to sacrifice his own needs for the care and comfort of his son, and of a son, who loves and admires his father because he understands what his father has done for him.

Just before David Lawrence departed for his mission to Switzerland, he and his father spent the day working the farm in Huntsville. Lawrence stopped to gaze at the farm for one last long look. His father said to him, "You're feeling it already, the loneliness." Not long after Lawrence arrived in France, David wrote to him, "Now that you are gone, Huntsville hasn't much attraction for either of us[25] [David and son Llewelyn]."[26]

Long-Distance Education

Because David was gone so often, letters were not simply a way to connect with his children and express his love and concern. Letters also became the medium through which David was an involved father and taught his children crucial principles that weighed on his mind. The following letter is an example of this long-distance teaching. The letter was written in May of 1909 from St. Johns, Arizona. Observe how David teaches Lawrence both academic and spiritual principles in the letter. At this time, Lawrence would have been eight years old:

> My dear Lawrence:
>
> When I came to St. Johns last Thursday, I found a sweet—loving letter from your mama waiting for me, and one from you, written so carefully and punctuated so correctly that I took pleasure in showing it to President Hart and others. I am so glad that you received all A's on your report card. I hope you will always get A's in everything you do, and especially in obeying Mama.
>
> When we were coming into St. Johns, we saw a horned toad. Have you ever seen the picture of one?
>
> Ask mama to show you a map of the United States, and then see if you can find St. Johns.
>
> They haven't had any rain here for several months, and they don't expect any until July 15th. Everything is dry, except in the towns where a little water comes from the creeks. The people haul their water in barrels, and water tanks. They are building reservoirs to hold all the water. When they get these built, they will have plenty of water, and then this will be good country.
>
> I am sending you and Llewelyn a nickel each. Please give Lou Jean and Mama a share of what you buy with the money, and tell

Lou Jean that papa has bought for her something very pretty. I bought it from an Indian.

There are many Indians and Mexicans in Arizona. . . .

Kiss Mama, Lou Jean, and Morgan, and Grandpa for me, and don't forget Josephine too.

With love to my boy, and best wishes for him always, I am

Your affectionate father
David O. McKay[27]

Years later, yet with the same sensitivity, David O. McKay apparently approached the subject of a girlfriend Lawrence must have had while serving as a missionary. He wrote his son the following letter:

One reference in your letter emphasizes the fact that you are just at a very impressionable age. I mention the fact simply to remind you that a young man's affections are very much like a young colt that is just being trained—He's alright as long as the trainer has a firm hold on the lines, and can keep him in the road. He wobbles around a good deal, but as long as he keeps going straight ahead, there's no need for worry. More than one pretty girl will make your heart go pit-a-pat; but keep your mind's eye on your missionary road.

You have some sweet brothers and sisters, and an ideal Mama, and they are all proud of their missionary brother and son. Such a family, I think makes life worth living. The success of parenthood may be rightly measured by the nobility of its sons and daughters! . . .

Please let us know about how much money you will need each month. A good way to ascertain this is to keep an accurate account of your daily expenditures. This is as good a training as keeping a diary.[28]

David O. McKay's letters to his children reveal that he was the consummate teacher. He often found ways to breach sensitive topics with his children, but his approach was with love, concern, and kindness. In the previous letter, we see his versatile ability to address topics from male-female relationships to basic accounting. From being away for so long, David learned to teach and influence his children through letters.

Father to All

A good measure of a father's spiritual progress is his care and concern for those around him. A successful father is not merely concerned with his own children, but he is concerned for the well-being of all children. President David O. McKay's son Edward shared the following experience to illustrate this point. He related that President McKay's car had been stolen.

> The police apprehended the thief, and it turned out to be a young boy of about twelve or thirteen. President McKay was asked if he wanted to prosecute the boy. He replied, "No, I will take care of it." He then interviewed the boy and asked him why he had stolen the car. The boy answered that he just wanted to try to drive a car. President McKay told him to come over to his house, and he would let him drive his car. He did that once a week for a long time. The young boy later became a police officer so that he could help others as David O. McKay had helped him.[29]

David O. McKay's care and concern blessed the lives of many children, not just his own. Because of the tender way he handled situations in and outside of his family, lives were changed and improved. For instance, instead of this young boy growing up to continually break the law, he chose to enforce it as his career. Moreover, when fathers care about their offspring, that love is most often reciprocated.[30] David O. McKay is an example to modern fathers on how to demonstrate care and concern. Another prophet, Joseph F. Smith, taught fathers how to demonstrate Christlike love to their children. He said:

> If you wish your children to be taught in the principles of the gospel, if you wish them to love the truth and understand it, if you wish them to be obedient to and united with you, love them! And prove to them that you do love them by your every word or act to them. . . . When you speak or talk to them, do it not in anger, do it not harshly, in a condemning spirit. Speak to them kindly; get them down and weep with them if necessary and get them to shed tears with you if possible. Soften their hearts; get them to feel tenderly

toward you. Use no lash and no violence . . . approach them with reason . . . with persuasion and love unfeigned. With these means, if you cannot gain your boys and your girls . . . there will be no means left in the world by which you can win them to yourselves. But, get them to love the gospel as you love it, to love one another as you love them; to love their parents as the parents love the children. You can't do it any other way. You can't do it by unkindness; you cannot do it by driving; our children are like we are; we couldn't be driven; we can't be driven now. . . . You can't force your boys, nor your girls into heaven. You may force them to hell, by using harsh means in the efforts to make them good, when you yourselves are not as good as you should be. . . . You can only correct your children by love, in kindness, by love unfeigned, by persuasion, and reason.[31]

David O. McKay believed these doctrines as taught by Joseph F. Smith. He modeled his life after these teachings, as his children have now passed them on to the next generation. This was a man who connected with his children by doing this with them; he demonstrated his love both verbally and physically and left no doubt in his children's minds that he loved them. When he corrected or disciplined his children, love ultimately prevailed. He taught his children the gospel of Jesus Christ by word and deed, and perhaps most importantly, he did all of these things with a loving and loyal wife at his side. Emma Ray helped David to temper his passions and to value relationships more than anything else.

Notes

1. David O. McKay, *Gospel Ideals*, 404.

2. President Ezra Taft Benson taught, "I am convinced that before a child can be influenced for good by his or her parents, there must be a demonstration of respect and love." Ezra Taft Benson, in Conference Report, April 1981, 46.

3. Robert D. Hales, "How Will Our Children Remember Us?" *Ensign*, November 1993, 8–9.

4. Brigham Young, *Discourses of Brigham Young*, comp. John A. Widtsoe (Salt Lake City: Deseret Book, 1954) 197–98.

5.   David C. Dollahite, Alan J. Hawkins, and Sean E. Brotherson, "Narrative Accounts, Generative Fathering, and Family Life Education," *Marriage and Family Review* 24, nos. 3–4 (1996): 349–68.

6.   David O. McKay, in Conference Report, April 1935, 112–13.

7.   Diaries of David O. McKay, April 1906 to June 1907, MS 668, box 4, folder 2, Marriott Library, 35.

8.   David O. McKay to Emma Ray Riggs, 23 June 1906, David O. McKay Family Papers, 1897–1954, MS 21606, box 1, folder 1, CHL.

9.   Diaries of David O. McKay, April 1906 to June 1907, MS 668, box 4, folder 2, Marriott Library, 36.

10. Ibid., 43.

11. Ibid.

12. Ibid.

13. Diaries of David O. McKay, February to December 1912, MS 668, box 5, folder 2, Marriott Library.

14. Ibid.

15. Ibid.

16. David recorded in his diary on 30 May 1932 that "Mama Ray, Ned, Bobby, and I visited the S.L. Cemetery, and placed flowers on Grandma Riggs and others graves. . . . We stopped at Royle's grave in the Ogden Cemetery, then continued on to Huntsville." This was twenty years after Royle's death. See *Diaries of David O. McKay*, January to November 1932, MS 668, box 7, folder 11, Marriott Library.

17. Llewelyn McKay, *Home Memories of President David O. McKay*, 75.

18. David O. McKay to Lou Jean McKay, 5 May 1921, David O. McKay Papers, MS 668, box 1, folder 5, Marriott Library.

19. He had been gone since early December of 1920.

20. David O. McKay to Emma Ray McKay, 4 July 1921, David O. McKay Papers, MS 668, box 1, folder 5, Marriott Library; underline and capitalization in original.

21. David O. McKay, in Conference Report, October 1917, 58.

22. David O. McKay to Emma Ray Riggs, 4 September 1909, David O. McKay Family Papers, 1897–1954, MS 21606, box 1, folder 1, CHL.

23. David Lawrence McKay, interview by Gordon Irving, James Moyle Oral History Program, Salt Lake City, January–May 1984, 22–23.

24. John Stewart, *Remembering the McKays*, 30.

25. It appears that once Lawrence arrived into the mission field, his family didn't hear from him for some time. One can speculate which of his parents would have been

more worried. The letter reads: "My Dear Son, David L: We have been wondering, almost every waking minute since you left, how you fared as a traveler. . . . Emma Ray was the first in the family to write you a letter. You will find it enclosed herewith. The love she expresses comes from her dear little heart; and that is love, my dear boy, that we all have for you. We are proud of your manliness, and grateful for your high ideals and keen sense of honor. Our confidence in you is absolute, and we feel sure that you will do your best to prove worthy of the Priesthood and to magnify every Calling you may receive as a true servant of the Lord. May Heaven's choicest blessings be yours during your entire mission!" McKay, *My Father, David O. McKay*, 109–10.

26. David O. McKay to David L. McKay, 29 October 1920, David O. McKay Papers, MS 668, box 2, folder 1, Marriott Library.

27. David O. McKay to David L. McKay, 22 May 1909, David O. McKay Family Papers, 1897–1954, MS 21606, box 1, folder 1, CHL.

28. David O. McKay to David L. McKay, 29 October 1920, David O. McKay Papers, MS 668, box 2, folder 1, Marriott Library.

29. Edward McKay, interview by Mary Jane Woodger, 30 June 1995.

30. David was in a serious car accident in Ogden Canyon while serving as a member of the Quorum of the Twelve Apostles. Someone had fastened a rope across the highway so drivers would not drive across the bridge because the river was so dangerous. David could not see the rope until it was too late. The rope smashed the car window and caught David under the chin, severing his lip, lacerating his face, knocking out his teeth, and breaking his jaw. On Sunday, Emma Ray gathered Lawrence, Llewelyn, and Lou Jean together to close their fast for their father and eat some breakfast before church. Llewelyn, who was ten at the time would have nothing to do with eating. Instead, he ran to the hospital to see his father. Before entering, he picked some bluebell and buttercup flowers for him. He then asked the nurse if he could see his father. The nurse then showed Llewelyn into the hospital room, where he placed the flowers in David's hand. Both the nurse and Llewelyn were crying. See Lou Jean McKay Blood, interview with Mary Jane Woodger, 8 August 1995.

31. Joseph F. Smith, *Gospel Doctrine* (Salt Lake City: Deseret Book, 1939), 316–17.

5

Disciplining Father

"If the home does not develop obedience, society will demand it and get it.
It is therefore better for the home with its kindness, sympathy, and understanding
to train the child in obedience rather than callously to leave him to the brutal and
unsympathetic discipline that society will impose."
—David O. McKay[1]

It is not easy being a parent. In fact, good parenting is one of the
most difficult challenges that most adults will ever face.[2] To be a
good parent takes time; it takes effort; it takes patience; it takes consistency; it takes perseverance; and it certainly requires unconditional
love. Nevertheless, there are many factors in dealing with children
that can be out of a parent's control. Often, while mothers and fathers
give parenting their best efforts, some children refuse to cooperate or
comply with their parents' teachings or values. Yes, there are some children who would give the very best parents a run for their money. Many
contemporary children are complex and can have a myriad of issues to
contend with. There is no "one-size-fits-all" formula for raising successful and well-adjusted children in our modern era.

Regarding parenting challenges, Elder Bruce C. Hafen shared the
following experience:

I once said in exasperation to my wife, Marie, "The Lord placed Adam and Eve on the earth as full-grown people. Why couldn't he have done that with this boy of ours, the one with the freckles and the unruly hair?" She replied, "The Lord gave us that child to make Christians out of us."

One night Marie exhausted herself for hours encouraging that child to finish a school assignment to build his own diorama of a Native American village on a cookie sheet. It was a test no hireling would have endured. At first he fought her efforts, but by bedtime, I saw him lay "his" diorama proudly on a counter. He started for his bed, then turned around, raced back across the room, and hugged his mother, grinning with his fourth-grade teeth. Later I asked Marie in complete awe, "How did you do it?" She said, "I just made up my mind that I couldn't leave him, no matter what." Then she added, "I didn't know I had it in me." She discovered deep, internal wellsprings of compassion because the bonds of her covenants gave her strength to lay down her life for her sheep, even an hour at a time.[3]

Being tired, worn out, frustrated, helpless, and even hopeless are sometimes common feelings for most parents. Indeed, as Sister Hafen stated, our children can make us into Christians, but they can also make us into something much less. Our challenge is to learn the lessons Heavenly Father intends for us and to become more like the Savior each day.

Furthermore, parenting is more than dealing with multifaceted personalities. To make the parenting issue even more complex, contemporary parents themselves are extremely busy. Between work responsibilities, Church assignments, basketball games, Cub Scout meetings, cheer practice, piano lessons, and swim meets, many Latter-day Saint families are experiencing a time famine. Arguably, both parents and children are busier now than at any time in our nation's history.

Years ago, a national opinion poll asked the question, "What is most important in life?" Ninety-six percent said, "To have a good family. And in a similar Gallup poll, eight of every ten people said family was one of the most or *the most* important facet of their lives."[4] Once again, most of us seem to understand what matters most in life. But there is often a disconnect between what we believe and how we live. And as was previously mentioned, even though most American parents value their families, too many are unwilling to be present with their families and spend time with their children consistently.

There are many consequences that can impact families when both parents and their children are excessively busy. For instance, when families are "over busy" and "over scheduled," children do not perform as well academically; they do not eat as nutritionally as they should; their self-worth can decrease; and the lack of relationships between parents and children could lead to all kinds of trouble.

However, there is one key consequence that may outweigh the other ones. When parents are busy, discipline, correction, and punishment often go by the wayside. With busy parents and a generation defined by excessive materialism, contemporary teens lack more discipline than any preceding generation. Indeed, discipline often takes a back seat when families are overscheduled and disconnected. Clinical psychologist Madeline Levine explained why:

> When time, not money, is the most valuable commodity in a household, then tasks that take a lot of time and effort with little apparent payback are often swept aside. . . . Busy parents already feel guilty about the little time they have to spend with their children. Few of them want to "waste time" in conflict and anger and as a result are often only too happy to sidestep discipline issues. The unfortunate result is that children do not learn how to take responsibility, control their impulses, or be thoughtful.[5]

Therefore, the discipline of children becomes one of the great challenges of our contemporary era. Too many parents are not willing to invest the time that it takes to discipline their children, nor do they understand how to discipline them. Perhaps some modern parents did not have adequate examples of good parenting, or, as Levine argues, they do not want to spend the little time they do have with their children arguing or fighting over cleaning a room or making a bed.

Unfortunately, this lack of discipline, combined with materialism, is not going to yield a generation of hardworking, productive adults.

Instead, the current lack of child discipline could ultimately unravel society as we know it. Modern children are excessively coddled, spoiled, and lazy compared to previous generations. The painful truth is that the prime responsibility of parents is not to gratify their children but to make certain "that they develop a repertoire of skills that will help them meet life's inevitable challenges and disappointments."[6]

President N. Eldon Tanner helped parents understand their duties when it comes to discipline when he stated, "Children must learn obedience, and parents must exact obedience from them. Love your children, let them know that you love them; but remember that it is no favor to a child to let him do things he should not do."[7] Indeed, children need love, but they also need to be taught to be responsible for their actions. *They need to be regulated so they can ultimately regulate themselves.* If parents do not teach or expect their children to be obedient, how will they learn later in life to respect or follow the counsel of their bishop? Their boss? How will they follow the instruction and counsel of their stake president? When their mission president asks them to serve in the most difficult area of the mission with a challenging companion, how will they do it? How will they learn to follow the prophet in these latter days? And perhaps most important, how will they ever learn to follow the quiet whisperings of the Holy Spirit if their parents have not taught them to be obedient? Children will never learn such lessons unless they are taught obedience, respect, and how to work in their own homes.

The Doctrine of Discipline

Decisions about discipline and how to administer consequences can cause some of the greatest challenges in parenting. The approach parents use to address a child's misbehavior speaks a great deal about how adults view their role as parents. The discipline methods used by parents are often a product of how they were parented, and they also point directly to what they expect of their children. In the heart of parenting, mothers and fathers must deal with different personalities, diverse temperaments, gender differences, and a host of other variables. No wonder President James E. Faust once declared:

> One of the most difficult parental challenges is to appropriately discipline children. Child rearing is so individualistic. Every child is different and unique. What works with one may not work with another. I do not know who is wise enough to say what discipline is too harsh and what is too lenient except the parents of the children themselves, who love them most. It is a matter of prayerful discernment for the parents. Certainly the overarching and undergirding principle is that the discipline of children must be motivated more by love than by punishment. Brigham Young counseled, "If you are ever called upon to chasten a person, never chasten beyond the balm you have within you to bind up" (in Journal of Discourses, 9:124–25). Direction and discipline are, however, certainly an indispensable part of child rearing.[8]

The teaching and disciplining of children is something that every Latter-day Saint prophet has addressed since the days of Joseph Smith. In fact, Joseph F. Smith stated that parents should "use no lash and no violence, but approach them with reason, with persuasion, and love unfeigned. The man that will be angry at his boy, and try to correct him while he is in anger, is in the greatest fault. . . . You can only correct your children by love, in kindness, by love unfeigned."[9] President Gordon B. Hinckley added his sentiment when he declared that "children don't need beating. They need love and encouragement."[10]

Elder David O. McKay taught the following in general conference:

> Our children are our most precious possessions; and the proper training of youth is the most important duty and obligation of society. . . . True education does not consist merely in the acquiring of a few facts of science, history, literature or art, but in the development of character. . . . True education trains in self-denial and self-mastery. True education regulates the temper, subdues passion and makes obedience to social laws and moral order a guiding principle of life.[11]

Indeed, President McKay believed that to discipline was to teach, and that the best teaching was to be done in the home. In fact, he viewed the duty for parents to instruct their children as "the highest assignment which the Lord can bestow upon man."[12] It was not the duty or obligation of the state, the school, or the Church to discipline children. That duty rested primarily on the shoulders of parents. It was President McKay's belief that if parents do not teach and require obedience in the home, then "society will demand it and get it."[13]

Parental Example

Perhaps more than any other parenting topic, President David O. McKay spoke most frequently regarding the need for parents to set a proper example for their children. It appears that he was keenly aware that teenagers can smell a hypocrite a mile away. President McKay often urged parents to be consistent with what they taught and how they behaved within the walls of their homes. As the President of the Church, he taught:

> Remember, fellow parents, that children are quick to detect insincerity, and they resent . . . false pretension. Parents, of all people on earth, should be honest with their children. Keep your promises to them and speak the truth always. Children are more influenced by the sermons you act than by sermons you preach. It is the consistent parent who gains the trust of his child. When children feel that you reciprocate their trust, they will not violate your confidence nor bring dishonor to your name.[14]

President McKay further taught that "behavior is caught, not taught," and that example is more potent than precept. It is the duty of parents to be what they would have their children become. Especially in aspects of courtesy, sincerity, temperance, and courage to choose the right in every situation.[15] David O. McKay would not teach these principles unless he lived them. Therefore, he would never require his children to do anything that he did not do himself. Because of this, his children admired him throughout their entire lives.

David O. McKay and family. (Courtesy of Intellectual Reserve, Inc.)

President McKay believed that the most effective way to "teach religion in the home was not by preaching but by living. If you would teach faith in God, show faith in him yourself; if you would teach prayer, pray yourself. Would you have [your children] temperate? Then you yourself refrain from intemperance."[16] And that he did. We can all learn from President McKay when it comes to example. He never required his children to live a principle or perform an act he was not willing to perform. Furthermore, he lived a life that inspired his children to want to be good. He always maintained a strong relationship with each of his children individually so that he could influence them. He further understood that rules without relationships inspire rebellion; therefore, he had a solid bond with each of his children.

Communicating Expectations

Perhaps only after the importance of parental example, the next step to successful child discipline is establishing clear-cut expectations. In this area alone, David and Emma Ray were laser focused. Their oldest son, Lawrence, reflected that his parents made their expectations perfectly clear, and they themselves

> were so self-disciplined that we were never confused by seeing them behave in a way different from the way we were supposed to behave. . . . Our parents' expectations provided the path for us to follow, and our love for them provided an irresistible motivation for us to walk that path. We learned to love them because they first dearly loved each other and us.[17]

Lawrence summarized, "Father expected the best. No one ever wanted to disappoint him."[18] Because of the great love and adoration the children had for their father, they wanted to please him by doing the right things. Often, parents shift the duty of the teaching and training of their children to the Church. However, former Primary general president Coleen K. Menlove reminded parents: "Casual, infrequent family prayers, scripture study, and family home evenings will not be enough to fortify our children. Where will children learn the gospel and standards such as chastity, integrity, and honesty if not at home? These values can be reinforced at church, but parents are the most capable and most effective in teaching them to their children."[19] Therefore, it is not the responsibility of institutions, including the Church, to teach and raise our children. Primarily, that job belongs to parents. The purpose of the Church, as Sister Menlove taught, is to reinforce what parents are teaching in the home.[20] Similarly, President David O. McKay declared, "There seems to be a growing tendency to shift this responsibility from the home to outside influences, such as the school and the church. Important as these outward influences are, they never can take the place of the influence of the mother and the father. Constant training, constant vigilance, companionship, being watchmen of our own children are necessary in order to keep our homes intact."[21]

Teaching Children Obedience

Aside from the practical experiences of raising seven children, President McKay had the opportunity to travel the world and observe parents from every walk of life. Many of these observations helped him formulate his opinions and passions regarding parenting. For example, on one of his train rides to a stake conference, he noticed the following and wrote to Emma Ray: "There is a lively two-year-old boy here in the car, and a mother who is constantly, constantly, constantly, saying, "Donald! . . . Donald, don't do that! . . . Donald, dear, come here!" etc., etc. And Donald does "that," and Donald doesn't come here, and so another future American citizen gets his first lessons in disregard for law and order. I am so glad for a loving wife who is also a wise mother, and I love her because she is both and more."[22]

Perhaps this experience and others like it inspired President McKay to say, "Parents should not fail to teach obedience to their children. Within the last decade there have been some rampant wild theories about the self-determination of children and the preservation of their individuality. Some of these theorists believe that children should be permitted to solve their own problems without guidance from parents. There is some virtue in this, but there is more error."[23]

The McKays' youngest son, Edward, recalled the time he was playing with matches behind the barn. His parents called him to come in, so he decided to hide the matches in the pocket of his overalls. In so doing, he failed to realize that the matches were visible. When President McKay asked his son what he was doing, he replied that he was simply playing in the barn. Then David asked Edward what was in his pocket. He said, "Cherries." David reached over towards his son and pulled a match out of his pocket. Edward reported, "I got a good spanking, not for playing with matches, but for lying."[24]

It is interesting that David O. McKay had a different way of disciplining each of his children. The children were not "scolded," but Lawrence reported that he and a few other siblings often got "the look." Apparently, David could give a complete sermon with a quick glance. Another brother, Bobby, required "the finger," which meant his father would tap him on the head with his finger and say, "Think about it, boy."[25]

As a father and priesthood leader, David believed that obedience should be taught in the home and that teaching obedience was most certainly a parental duty.[26] He often taught that if obedience was not taught in the home, society would demand it.[27] It would be much better to learn obedience from kind and loving parents by the family fireside, than have it enacted upon them by a police officer, school principal, coach, or any other who would not be as kind or understanding. President McKay further believed that there was a direct link to obedience and happiness. He declared that obedience is "heaven's first law, and it is the law of the home. There can be no true happiness in the home without obedience— obedience obtained, not through physical force, but through the divine element of love."[28] David O. McKay strongly believed that the best time to teach obedience to children is between the ages of two and four.[29] He was fond of quoting the popular proverb: "Train up a child in the way he should go: and when he is old, he will not depart from it."[30]

Teaching the Principle of Agency

Another aspect of discipline was teaching children the proper use of agency. The McKay children were taught true principles, but it was up to them to incorporate such teachings into their lives.[31] Regarding agency, David O. McKay taught that "next to the bestowal of life itself, the right to direct that life is God's greatest gift to man. . . . Freedom of choice is more to be treasured than any possession earth can give."[32] Lawrence shared the following experience:

> Father was a firm believer in free agency. I don't know that there was any proscription against face cards, but we never had any in our home. Llewelyn got a streak of independence when we were in high school and bought . . . a volume of Hoyle's rules and a deck of cards that he kept in his top drawer. I recall that Father once came in to look for something and found the deck of cards.
>
> "Whose are these?" he asked.
>
> "Mine," answered Llewelyn.
>
> Father looked at him, put them back in the top drawer, and walked out. He never referred to them or mentioned them again to Llewelyn; but as I recall, they didn't stay in the top drawer very long.[33]

David's daughter Emma Rae reported that when she was younger, she didn't want to attend church one particular Sunday. She asked her father, "Do I have to go to Sunday School?" David answered back, "You don't have to go! Just hurry and get your coat on so we won't be late." On another occasion, she wanted to play in a park on the Sabbath day. Her father responded, "You have six days in the week to play, but on Sunday we attend our Church meetings and do quiet things."[34] Yes, the McKay children had agency, but David understood that his job as a parent was to help his children exercise their agency in making correct choices!

Even though the McKay children had their agency, they also understood that their parents' expectations deserved consideration. The children were also keenly aware that there would be consequences for their choices. Even so, they wanted to follow their parents because of the respect they had for them. Interesting, however, was the fact that their father's Church callings made little difference in the choices the children made. It would seem that with an Apostle in the home, there would be much pressure to conform or to focus on appearance.

However, David O. McKay never expected his children to be perfect because of his high-profile position in the Church.

Lawrence was asked in an interview, "What was it like to be the son of a General Authority? Was that something you were proud of?" Lawrence responded by saying that having a father in the Church's limelight, or as a General Authority, was never emphasized in their family.[35] Lawrence further explained that his father rarely spoke of the Church or his duties as a member of the Quorum of the Twelve when he was home. It was as if David kept his life in two compartments: his church life and his family life.

It was not that he did not teach his children gospel principles— that surely happened. However, the "nitty-gritty" business details of governing the Church were never discussed. Lawrence explained, "He would never talk to us about Church affairs, but we all felt the importance of Church work."[36] It appeared that David wanted his children to grow up as normal as possible. He wanted them to have the same kind of life he did as a child—free to be young, to be taught in the framework of the gospel, to have a strong family life, and to learn to work. He didn't want his calling to cloud or negatively impact his children's lives.[37]

Through the proper exercise of agency, President McKay's choice was to be a righteous husband and father. Moreover, his commitment to the gospel, and his example in living it, inspired his children to do the same. Fathers today can make similar choices to bless the lives of their families. Perhaps to spend more time with the family, there is something to sacrifice, a skill or talent to improve upon, or a sin to repent of. There is always room for improvement in the gospel of Jesus Christ.

Never Repeat a Clear Command

One of McKay's core beliefs of child rearing was "Never give a child . . . a command that you cannot immediately see is carried out."[38] In harmony with that belief, he had another firm rule: "Never repeat a clear command. If you repeat it, the child will always wait for the repetition."[39] David O. McKay always tried to live the very things that he taught. Once his son Llewelyn was supposed to meet his father at 12:00 p.m. to go to Huntsville. Llewelyn made the mistake of showing up at 12:05 p.m. His father was gone.[40] Thus, the clear command was never repeated!

Lawrence learned a similar lesson. He remembers a ride to Huntsville in the surrey. He and his brother Llewelyn were sitting in the back seat and were doing what most brothers do—scuffling and goofing around. This was dangerous because such horseplay could lead to a child falling out of the carriage and under one of the large wheels. David O. McKay, with patience and calmness, asked his boys to stop. Unfortunately for them, they continued. That is when David removed his son Lawrence from the carriage. After the carriage moved on, Lawrence recalled:

> Walking up the hill, seeing the team and surrey going along, getting farther away by the minute. I was old enough to have walked the rest of the way and was certainly in no danger on the country roads of those times; but Father let me walk just far enough to contemplate the lesson in sufficient leisure, then stopped and waited for me. I was a much-chastened boy when I climbed back into the surrey. There was no more teasing and quarreling.[41]

In another account of the "surrey story" told years later, Lawrence recalled, "Mother prevailed on Father to stop at the top of the hill, I climbed in, and we were quiet from then on."[42] From that point on, young Lawrence McKay learned that when his father said something, he meant business.[43]

President McKay explained in general conference, "I believe firmly that parents . . . must get obedience from their children during the first five years of childhood. I believe that during that most important period of child life parents sow the seeds of obedience or disobedience. . . . Lovingly, kindly, but firmly, teach the child that there are rules in the house which should be obeyed."[44]

Even when President McKay was older, he never wavered on his stance. There was an incident where all of the family were gathered in the front room. One of the grandchildren, somewhere between the ages of three or four, was banging on the piano. Her mother asked her not to do it, but the child continued. That is when President McKay took matters into his own hands. He simply picked up his grand-daughter, put her in the next room, and shut the door.[45] The command was never repeated!

Freedom within Limits

President McKay taught, "The lesson of self-control should begin in childhood, in the home. Little children should have a sense of freedom to do as they wish up to a certain point. Beyond that point they cannot go, and that is when freedom interferes with the rights, comfort or convenience of another member of the family."[46]

David believed that everyone could learn much simply by observing monkeys. He and Emma Ray were at the San Diego Zoo watching a mother monkey with her newborn babe. She was guarding the baby monkey and protecting it from larger monkeys in the cage. However, the little monkey was free to do as it pleased. This tiny monkey hopped around, weak in its infancy, and began to grip the bars and attempted to climb around. When the baby monkey would reach a certain spot in the cage, the mother would simply reach up and pull the little infant back down to safety. President McKay continued, "When it got into a danger point, the mother instinctively guarded it and by action, said, 'Back this way.' And the babe was free again, but only within certain limits. I said to Sister McKay, 'There is a lesson of life in guiding children.'"[47]

This story helps illustrate David O. McKay's strong parenting belief: children are free to choose, but there are also boundaries they must respect. He well understood the difference between "agency" and "freedom"—two concepts misinterpreted by many contemporary parents. Freedom is to allow children to do whatever they please. Agency implies that children have choices, but there are consequences for the choices they make. David allowed his children to have their freedom, but there were always positive or negative consequences for their choices.

The Balance between Mother and Father

It appears that in the McKay household, David was certainly the disciplinarian, while Emma Ray was the nurturer. As with the "surrey story," it seemed that David was as adamant about having Lawrence "out" as Emma Ray was to having him "back in." Consider another example:

> The boys were playing baseball, not only an American pastime but a McKay family tradition. As will sometimes happen, one of the balls went right through a basement window. The guilty party went directly to his father and told him it was an accident and that he was sorry. David O. McKay replied, "I am sorry, too, but just being sorry will not repair the damage."
>
> The boy asked, "How much will a new window cost?"
>
> "I do not know," replied his father, "but we shall have a repairman come up and he can tell us the exact amount."
>
> The child offered, "I haven't much money, but I am willing to pay what I have."
>
> He was allowed to share in the expense, and when his mother remonstrated, "How could you take his money when he has such a small allowance?" David O. replied, "He has received a valuable lesson in the cost of keeping up a home, and now he has a monetary interest in this home which he will protect." It may have been a coincidence, but there were no more windows shattered by baseballs.[48]

If David needed to rebuke his children harshly, he could do it. However, he usually felt bad afterwards. On one occasion, Llewelyn disobeyed his mother, and David had zero tolerance for such discourtesy. He wrote in his diary: "Because of his disobedience to his mother, I reprimanded Llewelyn more severely than I ever have any other child. It grieved me severely to do it; well—I hope it will do good."[49] Since David recorded this incident in his diary, it must have weighed heavily on his mind.

At the same time, if a child deserved praise or commendation, David was often quick to compliment. For example, when Lawrence was six years old, he made the decision to cancel Christmas shopping with his parents to stay home and tend the baby—little Lou Jean. David recorded, "[Lawrence] had looked forward to this day to see the toys with mama and papa; but just at the last . . . circumstances made it necessary for him to stay with the baby. Lawrence is only six years but he will deny himself anytime for his parents. I record this just as one instance out of many."[50] From this simple reading, it is easy to detect that David was extremely proud of Lawrence for his willingness to sacrifice for his parents.

David believed that it was important to praise children. He adamantly believed that parents should never utter a cross word to each other, or to their children—especially while in public settings.[51] The late Truman G. Madsen—Brigham Young University professor, philosopher, and teacher—reported that he once attended a Sunday School meeting when David Lawrence McKay was serving as the general superintendent of Sunday School. Lawrence shared an experience with the teachers that evening that his father had related to him. Someone complained to President McKay that a particular Sunday School superintendent never began the Sunday School meetings on time. President McKay's response was to wait until this man *does* start the meeting on time, "even accidentally, and then praise him, fervently praise him for the one time he does it right, and you will see that he will keep doing it."[52] President McKay understood that rewarded behavior will continue. It was a principle he strongly embraced as a father. As a parent, David learned that if he was ever tempted to say something unkind or thoughtless to his children, he would put his tongue way back in his mouth and clamp his teeth down on it. He added, "And each time I did that, it was easier the next time not to say the unkind, hurtful thing."[53]

Sometimes the discipline of the children would lean more towards the justice side of David O. McKay, and most often the training and correcting would swing towards the mercy side of Emma Ray. Occasionally, David and Emma Ray would disagree on how to handle the discipline in the home. They never argued in front of the children, but it was obvious that they did have a few discussions behind closed doors.[54] They would come to an agreement and then present it to the children. This was a practice taught to both of them by David's father, who attributed his success as a parent to never disagreeing with his wife in front of the children. He told Emma Ray, "We go to our bedroom and talk things over, and when we come before our kiddies, we are of one mind."[55]

An example of this concept comes from an experience Lawrence shared:

> I noticed what could have been a difference of opinion one time when I saw an advertisement of a bargain joint subscription of *Youth's Companion* and the *Literary Digest*, both of which I wanted very much. I asked mother if we could subscribe, and thought she approved, but she said, "Ask your father." I did, and he said no. Mother looked at me but didn't say anything. I don't know what happened between them, but a few days later Father said, "Lawrence, you were asking about subscribing to the *Youth's Companion* and *Literary Digest*. That will be all right."[56]

One of the greatest revelations a man can receive is to listen to the counsel of his wife. It is a testament to David's character that he was also meek. For as strong as his opinions were, he humbled himself, listened to his wife, and repented of his mistakes. Emma Ray seems to have been able to "smooth him over" and bring him down to reality when that was necessary. Fathers who want to assist the next generation must communicate positively with their children. Strong fathers are not afraid to discipline their children. Instead, they understand that if they do not impose rules and regulations on their children, ultimately, society will. Better to be taught in the home—the laboratory of love—than to have our society impose discipline. President McKay warned "parents who fail to teach obedience to their children." He taught, "If your homes do not develop obedience society will demand it and get it. It is therefore better for the home, with its kindliness, sympathy, and understanding to train the child in obedience rather than callously to leave him to the brutal and unsympathetic discipline that society will impose if the home has not already fulfilled its obligation."[57]

David O. McKay disciplined his children with love, tenderness, and firmness. He is a powerful example of how to teach obedience to children in a loving environment. Fathers today can learn from his courage to discipline. David O. McKay further understood that to discipline is to teach, and that the prime responsibility of fathers is to be teachers and leaders.

Moreover, David O. McKay was a kind and nurturing father. He had a strong relationship with each of his children; he taught them about values and the commandments of God; he laughed with them and cried with them; he missed his children immensely when they left home. What President McKay taught as an Apostle, and ultimately as the President of the Church, about parenting and raising children corresponded perfectly with how he lived. The greatest gift this man gave to his family was his time—something he really didn't have. Yet, by giving his time to his family, he gave everything.

Notes

1. David O. McKay, in Conference Report, April 1955, 27.

2. Elder James E. Faust once declared, "In my opinion, the teaching, rearing, and training of children requires more intelligence, intuitive understanding, humility, strength, wisdom, spirituality, perseverance, and hard work than any other challenge we might have in life." James E. Faust, *Ensign*, November 1990, 32.

3. Bruce C. Hafen, "Covenant Marriage," *Ensign*, November 1996, 26.

4. Stinnett and DeFrain, *Secrets of Strong Families*, 3–4.

5. Madeline Levine, *The Price of Privilege*, 153.

6. Ibid., 76.

7. N. Eldon Tanner, in Conference Report, October 1977, 74.

8. James E. Faust, in Conference Report, October 1990, 41.

9. Joseph F. Smith, *Gospel Doctrine* (Salt Lake City: Deseret Book, 1963), 316–17.

10. Gordon B. Hinckley, "Save the Children," *Ensign*, November 1994, 52.

11. David O. McKay, in Conference Report, April 1928, 102.

12. In Conference Report, April 1955, 27.

13. Ibid.

14. David O. McKay, in Conference Report, April 1955, 26–27.

15. David O. McKay, in Conference Report, April 1935, 114.

16. David O. McKay, in Conference Report, April 1955, 27.

17. McKay, *My Father, David O. McKay*, 99.

18. As cited by Newell G. Bringhurst, "The Private Versus the Public David O. McKay: Profile of a Complex Personality," *Dialogue: A Journal of Mormon Thought* 31 (Fall 1998): 14.

19. Coleen Menlove, "A Voice of Gladness for our Children," *Ensign*, November 2002, 14.

20. In Doctrine and Covenants 68:25, the Lord instructs parents: "Inasmuch as parents have children in Zion . . . that teach them not to understand the doctrine of repentance, faith in Christ the Son of the living God, and of baptism and the gift of the Holy Ghost by the laying on of hands, when eight years old, the sin be upon the heads of the parents."

21. David O. McKay, in Conference Report, April 1969, 7.

22. David O. McKay to Emma Ray McKay, 22 May 1920, McKay Papers, box 1, folder 7, CHL.

23. Llewelyn McKay, *Home Memories of President David O. McKay*, 214.

24. Edward McKay, interview by Mary Jane Woodger, 30 June 1995.

25. Ibid.

26. David O. McKay, in Conference Report, April 1937, 30.

27. David O. McKay, in Conference Report, April 1967, 135.

28. David O. McKay, *Gospel Ideals*, 484.

29. David O. McKay, in Conference Report, April 1955, 27.

30. Proverbs 22:6.

31. Elder M. Russell Ballard taught, "Helping children learn how to make decisions requires that parents give them a measure of autonomy, dependent on the age and maturity of the child and the situation at hand. Parents need to give children choices and should be prepared to appropriately adjust some rules, thus preparing children for real world situations." M. Russell Ballard, "The Sacred Responsibilities of Parenthood," *Liahona*, March 2006, 10–17.

32. David O. McKay, in Conference Report, April 1950, 32.

33. McKay, *My Father, David O. McKay*, 102–3.

34. Emma Rae Ashton, interview by Mary Jane Woodger, 20 June 1995.

35. David L. McKay, interview by Gordon Irving, Salt Lake City, January–May 1984, James Moyle Oral History Program, MS 200 734, 24, CHL.

36. Ibid., 50.

37. If there was any pressure to be the "perfect family," it actually came from Emma Ray. One of her children reported, "Mother always told us that we had to set the example for everybody, because of Father's position. Father would never say that." Lawrence actually reported, "I got tired of Mother saying, 'You have to set an example.'" Perhaps Emma Ray felt more pressure as a parent than David did. Ibid., 22.

38. McKay, *My Father, David O. McKay*, 99.

39. Woodger, *David O. McKay*, 96.

40. Gunn McKay, interview by Mary Jane Woodger, 28 July 1995.

41. McKay, *My Father, David O. McKay*, 100; see also David L. McKay, interview by Gordon Irving, James Moyle Oral History Program, 13.

42. David L. McKay, interview by Gordon Irving, James Moyle Oral History Program, Salt Lake City, Utah, January–May 1984, 13.

43. David L. McKay, microfilm, address at a Luncheon of the 17th Annual Meeting of the Mormon History Association, 8 May 1982. MS 7013, CHL.

44. David O. McKay, in Conference Report, June 1919, 78.

45. Lou Jean McKay Blood, interview by Mary Jane Woodger, 8 August 1995.

46. David O. McKay, in Conference Report, September–October 1950, 165.

47. Ibid.

48. Jeanette Morrell McKay, *Highlights in the Life of President David O. McKay*, 44, 47.

49. Diaries of David O. McKay, August–December 1915, MS 668, box 5, folder 4, Marriott Library.

50. Diaries of David O. McKay, April 1906–June 1907, MS 668, box 4, folder 2, Marriott Library, 105.

51. David O. McKay, in Conference Report, October 1967, 149.

52. Truman G. Madsen, *The Presidents of the Church* (Salt Lake City: Deseret Book, 2004), 247.

53. As cited in Stephen R. Covey, *Spiritual Roots of Human Relations* (Salt Lake City: Deseret Book, 1993), 123.

54. David Lawrence McKay, interview by Gordon Irving, James Moyle Oral History Program, Salt Lake City, January–May 1984, 133.

55. Emma Ray McKay, "The Art of Rearing Children Peacefully," *Brigham Young University Speeches of the Year*, 12 April 1952, 9.

56. David Lawrence McKay, "Remembering Father and Mother, President David O. McKay, and Sister Emma Ray Riggs McKay," *Ensign*, August 1984, 34–36.

57. David O. McKay, *The Responsibility of Parents to Their Children* (Salt Lake City: The Church of Jesus Christ of Latter-day Saints, n.d.), 1.

6

Consecration and Sacrifice

"No man or woman can create a true home who is not willing in the outset to embrace life heroically, to encounter labor and sacrifice. Only to such can this divinest power be given to create on earth that which is the nearest image of heaven."
—David O. McKay[1]

Consecration involves "the call and capacity to dedicate one's time, talents, resources, and energies to the well-being of the next generation."[2] In this sense, for fathers to be consecrated means they are wholly dedicated to their families and willing to make the necessary sacrifices for their children. And although it may surprise some, most children want to have a relationship with their fathers.

It is interesting to note that in 1924, 63 percent of teenagers in a major city reported that the most desirable attribute in a father is that he spends time with his children; by 1977, that figure rose to 68 percent. Unquestionably, children appreciate and desire fathers who will take time to be with them and invest in them.[3] Some of the most cherished memories for children and their fathers include going on family vacations, camping together, making pinewood derby cars, and hanging the Christmas lights. When fathers can spend one-on-one time with their children, they send a powerful message regarding what the father values the most. Elder Dallin H. Oaks shared the following experience:

> A friend took his young family on a series of summer vacation trips, including visits to memorable historic sites. At the end of the summer he asked his teenage son which of these good summer activities he enjoyed most. The father learned from the reply, and so did those he told of it. "The thing I liked best this summer," the boy replied, "was the night you and I laid on the lawn and looked at the stars and talked." Super family activities may be good for children, but they are not always better than one-on-one time with a loving parent.[4]

Strong fathers do not leave family togetherness to chance. They make things happen, and they make time for their families. Unfortunately, many American fathers have accepted the phrase, "Well, it's not the *quantity* of time I am spending with my children, but the *quality* of time."[5] Therefore, such fathers have justified their absence in the name of quality activities each month. Unfortunately, such an investment yields mediocre results at best. A notable family therapist, George Rekers, has explained the quantity versus quality dilemma in a striking way: Imagine that you have gone to a very nice gourmet restaurant to treat yourself to a steak, even though it costs $18.00. The steak arrives on an expensive china plate, served with flair by an impeccably dressed waiter. You note with shock and dismay that the steak is a one-inch cube. In horror, you question the waiter, who assures you that the quality is what counts and this steak is *the best*. But if you're hungry, you'll know that the quantity also counts.[6]

In reality, strong fathers agree that there must be both quality time and quantity of time devoted to children. However, the quantity must be there for the quality to have an impact. President Howard W. Hunter taught fathers in a priesthood session of general conference, "Effective family leadership . . . requires both quantity and quality time. The teaching and governance of the family must not be left to your wife alone, to society, to school, or even the Church."[7]

Relationships cannot be built while constantly checking the clock, nor can they be developed on the father's schedule alone. Often, children approach their parents at the most inopportune times. Effective and nurturing fathers will make time for their children, even if it is not convenient for them to do so.

Love Spelled T-I-M-E

One of Satan's greatest tools among active and faithful Latter-day Saints is distraction. If he can pull us just a few degrees off course, he could gradually wreak havoc on our lives. In describing the busy and chaotic world in which we live, Sheri Dew explained:

> Lucifer works hard to undermine our innate tendency to nurture and care for others. He wants us to become separated from each other. Voice messaging and pagers are efficient, but they don't replace a listening ear and a caring heart. If the adversary ... can keep us so busy running from one commitment to another that we no longer have time for each other, he has made great strides towards neutralizing the strength and influence that we have. We need each other. We need each other's testimonies and strength, each other's confidence and support, understanding and compassion.... Lucifer would have us so busy—with the details swirling around family, friends, careers, and every soccer league in town—that there's not time to actually live the gospel. No time to fast and pray, to immerse ourselves in the scriptures, to worship in the temple—all the things we need to do to "study for our mortal test." In other words, he wants us to be a little more concerned with the world than with the gospel, a little more interested in life today than in life forever.[8]

If we are not careful, busyness can destroy our family relationships and erode our souls. David O. McKay provides a tremendous example of how fathers can balance their lives and consecrate their efforts towards their children. Despite his busy schedule, President McKay was a father who found ways to make time for his children. He understood that to be an effective father, he would often have to sacrifice his time and his interests. In a general conference, President McKay explained, "Children take time, trouble, and more patience than we usually have. They interfere with freedom, good times, and luxury, but children are the real purpose behind marriage."[9] Although parenthood does requires time, trouble, and patience, President McKay recognized that children are our most important possessions.[10] Therefore, he tried his best to spend time with his own children. Although this was not easy to do, President McKay found ways to make it happen.

Taking His Children on Church Trips

Perhaps the most significant way David O. McKay was able to spend time with his children was by taking them with him on his stake conference assignments. This was a practice he engaged in as often as the occasion permitted. For example, on Friday, 22 March 1907, David was on his way to a stake conference in Cache Valley. He wrote in his diary, "Took Lawrence my little boy with me. This was his first initial trip. I hope to take him as often as I can."[11] After the conference concluded, David reported, "We had an excellent conference. Lawrence has been a little hero."[12] It appears that David and Lawrence traveled to Logan by carriage, because he reports that Lawrence survived the wintery ride all right.[13]

Because Lawrence behaved so well, it appears that David became quite daring about two months later. On Sunday, 26 May 1907, he reported that he boarded the 12:10 p.m. train for Logan to attend the baccalaureate exercises at Brigham Young College. "Took Lawrence and Llewellyn with me. They were intensely interested as well as interesting."[14] Even though David points out that his boys were "interesting," they must have been quite well-behaved, because he continued to take them on Church assignments throughout their lives.

Lawrence further explained, "Because the railroads offered half-priced tickets to children under the age of eight,[15] Father made a point of taking one of us children with him on his conference assignments when it was practical."[16] On these trips, David had plenty of time to connect with his children. He would also use these outings to teach his children as much as he could about the Church, the gospel, and even about the world in general. He also enjoyed taking his children to historical sites and other places of interest.

In August of 1910, just before the start of the school year, David took Lawrence with him to a stake conference in Taber, Alberta, Canada. On that trip, Lawrence wrote home to his mother and reported that he was having a great time fishing and camping with his father.[17] Furthermore, on their way to Canada, the train made a stop in Butte, Montana. This gave David and his oldest son an opportunity to attend a circus while they were passing through town.[18]

In October of the same year, David took Llewelyn with him to a stake conference in the San Francisco area. David made the time to take his son to the Golden Gate Park, where they saw buffalo and slid down a slippery wood slide together. They also went down to cliff rocks, where they saw big sea lions and seagulls. They visited the library and studied animals by looking at their pictures in encyclopedias and other books. Afterwards, they went to the zoo and located the very animals they had studied.[19] On this same trip, David wrote to Emma Ray and gave her this report:

> Llewelyn is fine, and enjoying his trip immensely, as you will see by his letter. He is a great boy and attracts people to him, even in the street car, when there is no occasion to notice him. Night before last in the barber shop, he was the center of attraction. Almost as soon as I was in my chair, he had been invited to sit in another, and was given an electronic massage and a hair comb.... Here at the hotel, yesterday, the manager of the café made this remark to Pres. Robinson, referring to Llewelyn: "He's the best trained kid that was ever in this hotel; I'll bet that he has a fine mother! When this was told to me, I answered, "You are right—he has a fine mother, the best in the world."[20]

Trips to the Farm

It seemed that David made it a practice to take a child with him wherever he traveled, whenever he could. This rule not only applied to stake conference visits but even when David was home. For example, he would often take his children with him on personal trips—especially when he had to check on the farm. While home one weekend, he recorded in his journal, "Drove to Huntsville. Cut hay. Took Llewelyn with me and we stayed overnight."[21] He was constantly taking his children, most often one at a time, with him to Huntsville. David also enjoyed taking his children to the circus, on joy rides in the car, and on vacations.[22]

Historian Francis Gibbons commented on David's priorities:

> Often a man confronted with such multiple demands on his time will sacrifice family needs to other responsibilities. David O. McKay never did so. He endeavored to interweave his church, professional, and business activities with those of his family. This he did by taking family members with him when he performed other duties, as we have already seen, and as we shall see him do in his later career to even greater degree. And the time he did spend with his family was always quality time with recreational activities being planned so as to involve the entire family, if possible.[23]

President McKay didn't seem to believe in relaxing much. When he had any free time, he bolted for the family farm in Huntsville, seizing opportunities to work with his boys. He even reminded Emma Ray in a letter that if the choice was between working at the farm or going to the Saltair (a resort on the banks of the Great Salt Lake) to enjoy some leisure time, he would choose the farm—and he did on many occasions.[24] Lawrence recalled that they only went on one camping trip:

> The only "camping" trip I recall was one July when the General Authorities had their vacation, and Mother, for some reason, needed to be in Ogden. He took Llewelyn and me, then in High School, on what he called a picnic. He put hay and quilts for bedding in the wagon and drove us to Dry Hollow. We worked all that day, slept at night in the wagon, and worked the next day, bringing a ditch from the spring down to the farm. When we were digging potatoes with him, he sang the beautiful Samoan farewell song, "Tofa My Felina" (Good-bye, My Friend), one of the cherished souvenirs he brought with him from his tour around the world. We also played hard on the farm. It was a tradition to make hay on the Fourth and the Twenty-fourth of July. We would begin early in the morning, work hard, eat a gigantic dinner at midday and, later in the afternoon, play an all-family baseball game with everyone—even little children participating.[25]

Modeling Consecration and Work

David O. McKay believed that one of the greatest legacies he could pass down to his children was a strong work ethic.[26] He wanted his children to consecrate their lives to the cause of the family and the Church. He taught, "This religion teaches men to work. The idler has no place in the Church."[27] David did not need to preach many sermons to his children on the subject of hard work; instead, he set an example by his strong work ethic. He worked beside his children and grandchildren and taught them how to work hard. In fact, he connected to his children through working. As his two oldest sons approached adulthood, he wrote the following to Lawrence. At the time, David was in the First Presidency, and he was writing from Santa Monica, California:

> I am glad you are looking after matters in Huntsville. That was good work you and Llewelyn did in shutting out the cattle from the self-feeder. It is a source of true satisfaction to see you boys go right ahead with the work without being told. With the amount of other obligations and duties on my hands now, I think I shall have to shift the running of the farm on the shoulders of my boys. I am mighty thankful, too, that we have boys intelligent and industrious enough to run it.[28]

As was previously mentioned, President McKay continued to work hard on the farm even in his twilight years. He would take his younger children, Emma Rae (20), Ned (16), and Bobby (11), to Huntsville to "enjoy the winter snow and to work off some of their nervous energy."[29] After his older sons were gone from home, President McKay would take Ned and Bobby to the farm where they would work long days.[30] On one of these weekend "respites," they planted "three-fourths of an acre of potatoes."[31] Like other men who became prophets, David O. McKay seemed to relax with his children by working with them. However, besides reading to them and working with them, he enjoyed playing a good game of baseball with them when he could.[32]

Living the Law of Sacrifice

David O. McKay made sacrifices for his children so that their lives would be better and happier. This was a man who rarely did what he wanted to do, with the exception of farm work. There is little evidence that David O. McKay golfed, fished, or pursued hobbies, though he very well could have. Similarly, there is little evidence that he spent much of his time in idle pursuits. Instead, his family was his hobby and his first priority. No wonder he taught, "When one puts business or pleasure above his home, he that moment starts on the down grade to soul ruin. The loss of fortune is nothing compared with the loss of home."[33] This was a man who strived to never put anything before his wife or children. Work was one of the ways he connected with his children.

When he was not engaged in his heavy work responsibilities, he was with his family. If he was not with his family, then most likely he was involved in his work responsibilities. Those seemed to be his only two options. David O. McKay understood that children are what family life is all about. This man always longed to be with his family.

On the night of 7 December 1920, he wrote from a ship to his Emma Ray, "My most fervent prayer to our Heavenly Father is that He will keep you and our beloved children in perfect health until we meet again. To be reunited as a loving family, each one healthy, virtuous, and true, is the one great blessing I pray to enjoy!"[34] It seemed that President McKay closed most of his letters with similar sentiments.

As President McKay taught, successful fathers find ways to spend time with their children. They make the necessary sacrifices so that they can be involved in their children's lives. Contemporary fathers would do well to adjust their schedules and determine how they can be more involved in the lives of their children. If fathers choose to ignore this responsibility, they must be prepared for the consequences that will inevitably follow. Michael Gurian, the author of *The Wonder of Boys*, explained, "If the father, tired from work, spends just ten minutes with the boy, or a half hour, both will feel refueled. If, whether in the boy's infancy or later in life, the father doesn't spend the minimal amount of time with his child, he'll actually end up spending more than that amount of energy dealing with his son's anger, rejection, and abandonment throughout an evening, weekend, or lifetime."[35]

To be a parent is to make sacrifices. Wives and children need to know that their husbands and fathers are willing to give up their own interests and pursuits for their well-being. These sacrifices will often include time, energy, and means. Such sacrifices are often as simple as attending children's activities, coaching their teams, or taking trips together. Sometimes, fathers will be required to place much more on the altar. Some men will turn down job opportunities or give up their personal interests or hobbies so their families can flourish. Years ago, the First Presidency declared to fathers, "As a leader in your home, you plan and sacrifice to achieve the blessing of a unified and happy family. To do all of this requires that you live a family-centered life."[36] David O. McKay understood the need to make sacrifices so that his family could thrive. Mostly, he gave of himself. This man never seemed to mind making sacrifices for his family.

Notes

1. David O. McKay, in Conference Report, April 1945, 144.

2. Dollahite, Hawkins, and Brotherson, "Fatherwork: A Conceptual Ethic of Fathering as Generative Work," 31.

3. James Garbarino, "Reinventing Fatherhood," *Families in Society* 74 (January 1993): 51–54.

4. Dallin H. Oaks, "Good, Better, Best," in Conference Report, 6–7 October 2007, 111.

5. Nick Stinnett and John Defrain, *Secrets of Strong Families* (Little Brown & Co., 1985).

6. Ibid., 83.

7. Howard W. Hunter, in Conference Report, October 1994, 68.

8. Sheri Dew, *No Doubt About It* (Salt Lake City: Deseret Book, 2001), 97–98.

9. David O. McKay, in Conference Report, April 1956, 9.

10. He declared in his inaugural year as the President of the Church that "our country's most precious possession is not our vast acres of range land supporting flocks and herds; not productive farms—not our forests; not our mines nor oil wells producing fabulous wealth—our country's greatest resource is our children, our

young men and women whose characters will largely determine our nation's future." David O. McKay, in Conference Report, October 1951, 5.

11. Diaries of David O. McKay, April 1906 to June 1907, MS 668, box 4, folder 1, Marriott Library, 109.

12. Ibid., 113.

13. Ibid., 114.

14. Ibid., 137.

15. In another interview, Lawrence reported that the half-priced rates were for children up to twelve years of age.

16. McKay, *My Father, David O. McKay*, 45–46.

17. David Lawrence McKay to Emma Ray Riggs, 20 August 1910, David O. McKay Family Papers, 1897–1954, MS 21606, box 1, folder 1, CHL.

18. David O. McKay to Emma Ray McKay, 16 August 1910, David O. McKay Family Papers, 1897–1954, MS 21606, box 1, folder 1, CHL.

19. David O. McKay to Emma Ray McKay, 26 October 1910, David O. McKay Family Papers, 1897–1954, MS 21606, box 1, folder 1, CHL.

20. David O. McKay to Emma Ray McKay, 26 October 1910, David O. McKay Family Papers, 1897–1954, MS 21606, box 1, folder 1, CHL.

21. Gibbons, *David O. McKay*, 75.

22. Diaries of David O. McKay, April 1906 to June 1907, MS 668, box 4, folder 2, Marriott Library, 37.

23. A favorite group diversion in 1907 was buggy riding. On 17 July 1907, David wrote, "In the evening took Ray and the Babes out buggy riding. Later we packed up ready for my trip." Gibbons, *David O. McKay*, 76.

24. David O. McKay to Emma Ray McKay, 15 September 1921, David O. McKay Papers, MS 668, box 1, folder 6, Marriott Library.

25. McKay, *My Father, David O. McKay*, 65–66. The song is titled "Tofa Mai Feleni."

26. At the October 1909 general conference, David taught that one of the predominating elements of salvation was work. "Work in the home! Work; legitimate work, in the avenues of life! Work, legitimate work in the social world." David O. McKay, in Conference Report, October 1909, 90.

27. David O. McKay, *Instructor*, July 1962, 218.

28. David O. McKay to David Lawrence McKay, 7 December 1918, David O. McKay Family Papers, 1897–1954, MS 21606, box 1, folder 1, CHL.

29. Gibbons, *David O. McKay*, 131.

30. At this point in his life, David O. McKay was nearly sixty years old. There are not many sixty-year-old men today who could work as he did.

31. Gibbons, *David O. McKay*, 143.

32. Woodger, *David O. McKay: Beloved Prophet* (American Fork, UT: Covenant Communications, 2004), 94.

33. David O. McKay, in Conference Report, April 1935, 115.

34. David O. McKay to Emma Ray McKay, 8 December 1910, David O. McKay Papers, MS 668, box 1, folder 4, Marriott Library.

35. Michael Gurian, *The Wonder of Boys* (New York: Putnam Books, 1996), 116.

36. *Father, Consider Your Ways* (Salt Lake City: The Church of Jesus Christ of Latter-day Saints, 1973), 4–5.

7

Building
Relationships

"One of the paramount duties, I might say the paramount duty, of parents is
to win and merit the confidence and respect of their children."
—David O. McKay[1]

Successful fathers build strong, lasting emotional bonds with their children. Such relationships benefit both father and child. Urie Brofenbrenner, former child development psychologist, explained:

> Every child should spend a substantial amount of time with somebody who's crazy about him or her. . . . There has to be at least one person who has an irrational involvement with that child, someone who thinks that kid is more important than other people's kids, someone who's in love with him or her, and whom he or she loves in return. . . . You can't pay a [person] to do what a [parent] will do for free.[2]

In order for fathers to connect with their children, of course they must know their child, but they most also love their child the way he or she wants to be loved. In other words, it's not enough for fathers to attempt to connect with their children by doing only what they like to do. Fathers must also attempt to connect with their children in the manner the child prefers. For example, some fathers may try to connect with a child by shooting guns or playing a sport. However, if the child would rather attend a concert or build something with tools, then a father wanting to bond through shooting or sports will gain little traction with that child. Hence, fathers *must* connect with their children at their level. Psychologist Madeline Levine explained:

> There are no shortcuts to knowing our children well. Warmth is cultivated when we take time, when we linger with our children, when we get to know them in the most intimate and specific ways we can. Know what delights your particular child or what disappoints her and what turns her off. Does your daughter love poetry and hate science fiction? Does your son keep the television on all night because he likes the background noise or because he's afraid of the dark?
>
> Being truly connected with our children means knowing and valuing the unique, idiosyncratic, one-in-a-trillion child who stands in front of us. Reinforce your love and appreciation as often as you can. Make sure your child knows that, if given a choice of all the children in the world, he or she is the one you would choose.[3]

To connect with a child is "to form healthy lasting attachments with a child."[4] A father cannot connect with his children unless he understands his children and seeks to meet their needs. Successful fathers establish bonds with their children by doing things with them.[5] Moreover, "Father-child relationships are strengthened when fathers competently respond to a child's needs."[6] When there is connection between fathers and their children, there is also the opportunity to influence, teach, and guide them. A father who has no relationship with his children will have little ability to influence them for good or teach them the things that matter. David O. McKay was a father who was connected to his children both emotionally and spiritually. The deep connection he had with his children serves as an example to all fathers on how to build strong parent-child relationships.

A Sixth Sense

David O. McKay seemed to have a sixth sense when it came to his children. As was mentioned in a previous chapter, when something was wrong with them, he seemed to be able to detect it—regardless of how far away he was from his family. For example, on his world tour, when he was over five thousand miles away from home, he awoke on the morning of 30 December 1920 concerned about the health of his young daughter Emma Rae. He wrote in his diary later that evening, "Awoke this morning with depressed feeling regarding my little sunshine Emma Rae. Have tried in vain to throw it off, thinking it the result of a fitful sleep."[7] As it turned out, nothing was wrong with Emma Rae. She wasn't sick after all, but another child was. In fact, David received two letters from his wife, Emma Ray, informing him that "Neddy Boy" had been quite sick. Upon hearing this news, David recorded in his diary, "The news of Neddy Boy's illness made me quite downhearted; but I found relief in a supplication to the Lord, which, I feel sure he would answer in blessings on my Little Ones."[8] When things were not right at home, David sensed it.

As an Apostle many miles from home, often all David could do was rely on the Lord for peace and comfort when his children were sick. Aside from the many emotions this may have stirred, it must have been a helpless feeling to say the least. When they were sick or otherwise afflicted, David was affected as well. He once reported in his diary that it was a gloomy day for him because Ned was sick.[9] David had such a strong relationship with his children that he actually suffered when they suffered. His concern toward his suffering children, as well as his joy in their happiness, is evidence of a strong bond.

Homesick Traveler

While on the world tour in Tonga, David had several bouts with severe homesickness. It was something he struggled with constantly while he was away from his loved ones. Because of his strong connection with his family, there was deep and significant emotional pain when he was far away from them. On 2 June 1921, he spent most of the day in the mission home, writing letters to home and fighting homesickness—he had not heard from Emma Ray since March. He wrote, "Ray promised to cable if anything should go wrong at home, so I conclude that no word is good word."[10] Apparently, the theory that "no news is good news" didn't hold much water. When he went for long periods of time without hearing from Emma Ray, it was very difficult for him. Especially on these long trips, David constantly thought of his wife, his children, and Huntsville. His homesickness is a continual theme in his diaries.

The only remedy for this weary traveler, short of taking a transcontinental jet straight to Ogden, was a message he received from Emma Ray just a few days later. On 28 June 1921, he received a cablegram from Emma Ray that simply read, "Letter received—Have written—I miss you very, very much." In response to this short message, David recorded in his diary,

> As this was the first word from my Loved Ones since I left home, March 26th, it seemed the dearest message I've ever received in my life. "Everybody all well!" What more comforting words would a traveler have than these? Unless it be those from his sweetheart, "I miss you very, very much"! I felt it no weakness to let tears of joy express my appreciation.[11]

Connection through Emulation

President McKay observed, "Children are more influenced by sermons you act than by the sermons you preach."[12] Indeed, strong fathers will recognize that how they live is their most powerful sermon. Since children are always watching, how a father acts is much more significant than what he preaches or teaches. Usually, evidence of a strong, healthy relationship between a father and his children is emulation. Most of us want to be like the people we love and admire. Emulation implies admiration and relationship, and David's children wanted to be just like him. He taught, "Our debt to our parents is unpayable except in one way, and that is by emulating their ideals and bringing joy to them in their old age."[13]

For example, one of David's young sons was visiting the home of his grandfather. It was springtime, and workmen occupied the home as they were cleaning the house and hanging wallpaper. A particular workman asked the young McKay, "When you are a man, would you like to be a painter and paper-hanger?" Without any hesitation, the child answered, "No, sir." The workman then asked, "Then what would you like to be?" The boy promptly responded, "I should like to be a 'Twelve Apostle.'"[14] Obviously this young boy looked up to his father, who at the time was serving in the Quorum of the Twelve Apostles.

Connection with Humor

Another way through which a father can connect with his children is with humor. A successful father will not take himself too seriously. Moreover, he will create a fun, enjoyable, happy atmosphere in the home. David O. McKay loved to laugh, and he forged family relationships through the medium of humor. Daughter Lou Jean recalled: "Father was not at all serious. . . . He was fun at the dinner table. When I was at the University, father would come home for dinner. He wanted a happy dinner, no sad stories. At the office he would get a Scottish joke. He would come home and have us laughing. He wanted us to be happy. When he came home, he played games with us. We loved that. We loved our father, he was such a darling with us. He wasn't strict. He taught us lessons. He meant what he said and we obeyed him."[15]

Lawrence remembered that his father always seemed to have a humorous story to tell, but he was careful not to use humor inappropriately, especially at the expense of another family member. However, there was one exception to this rule. When the family was in Huntsville one summer, David sent Lawrence out to the garden to get a head of lettuce. Instead, Lawrence returned with a head of cabbage. His father said, "That's not the only cabbage head you brought back."[16] Lawrence may have been the only one not laughing after that.

Even when President McKay became older, his humor never left him. Lawrence had shoveled some snow off the walks at the cottage in Huntsville. As he was assisting his father down the sidewalk, President McKay slipped, bumped into Lawrence, and took them both down like bowling pins. Both President McKay and Lawrence were laughing hysterically. Lawrence said, "Father was like a boy in his ability to enjoy such things."[17]

President McKay once taught, "The dearest possession a man has is his family. In the divine assurance that family ties may transcend the boundaries of death, and may continue throughout endless ages of eternity, I find supreme consolation and inspiration."[18] David certainly treated his children as his dearest possessions. He must have believed that laughing together was one way to make lasting memories.

One on One

Speaking of the importance of one-on-one relationships in the family, Dr. Stephen R. Covey pointed out that "these one-on-ones are where most of the real work of the family is done. This is where there is the deepest nurturing of heart and soul. This is where the most significant sharing, the most profound teaching, the deepest bonding takes place."[19] David learned from his educational career that a parent must have a relationship with his or her children if he or she wants to teach or influence them. The future prophet also understood how important it is to have a significant relationship with each child individually. Often, these bonds were revealed through many of the letters that David wrote to his children, especially as they left for college, went on missions, and got married.

For example, in a letter he wrote to Emma Ray regarding their daughter Lou Jean's upcoming marriage, he related: "I have just finished a letter to Lou Jean. Tears began to blur my eyes, so I had to bring it to an abrupt close. As I began writing, the full realization of the fact that the first one of our darlings to leave us to make a home for herself flooded my soul to overflowing—I confess that this first break in our lovely, charming family group, gives me a feeling in my heart akin to a pang."[20]

In another letter from Tucson, Arizona, in 1925, David wrote to Emma Ray, "Thus far, at least we have had no reason to be ashamed of any of our Treasures. From David L. to 'Bobbie,' they are all Jewels of the finest grade. Thanks to their perfect little Mother!"[21] He highlighted the word "treasures" in the letter—a term of endearment from a father who deeply loved his children.

On a trip to southern Arizona, David advised Emma Ray, "Keep the boys busy, and in your company as much as possible, especially Lawrence. He needs more of our companionship. I wish he were with me on this trip. He would enjoy it and profit by it, and I should not be so lonesome."[22] Indeed, David was connected to his children emotionally, and it pained his heart to be gone from them as often as he was.

His children shared this same bond or connection with their father. For example, when Lawrence was a teenager, he wrote a letter to his father and gave him the entire play-by-play, inning-by-inning performance of a baseball game between Murray and Ogden, with a complete description of a fight that broke out after the game.[23] Likewise, Llewelyn once wrote his father and reported that since both David and Emma Ray were gone on this particular trip, the children had "cake" for dinner. He closed his letter with a postscript: "Please write and tell us about the first time you play golf."[24] It appears that part of David's relationship with his sons was built on sports talk—a language they all understood. Perhaps there were many discussions on the farm in Huntsville about baseball and other sports.

Heart Petals

The year 1922 was a busy time for the McKay clan. Lawrence was serving as a missionary in France, and Llewelyn had just commenced his service in the Swiss-German Mission. Meanwhile, the rest of the family was in Liverpool after David accepted a call from President Heber J. Grant to serve as the president of the European Mission. The McKays had sold their longtime home in Odgen, and now it appeared that stability had left them. Llewelyn was extremely homesick and wrote a rather sad letter to David about his feelings. One day, while

David O. McKay as president of the European Mission. (Courtesy of Intellectual Reserve, Inc.)

David O. McKay was riding a train between Liverpool and London, he penned the following poem for Llewelyn:

Dear Llewelyn:

'I'd give part of Germany; yes, all of it, too,
For just one wee hug of dear Bobbie and you';
So runs your letter to Mother this day,
The first she's received since you sailed away.
You'd have thought that a rainstorm had burst, as she read,
So fast down her sweet face the large teardrops sped.
'Twas her love sending answer in reciprocal joy,
Saying, 'I'd give the world to hug you, my boy!' . . .
Old Time passes quickly—too quickly, my lad,
As into our lives he throws good and bad;
'Twill be but a span ere your wish you'll possess,
And Mother and 'Bobbie' you'll fondly caress.
Be yours then to say, in that moment of bliss,
As loved ones you greet with a pure loving kiss:
'Though waves of temptation around me did roll,
They but tempered my manhood; untainted's my soul!'[25]

In this case, although busy with mission responsibilities, David O. McKay took the opportunity to connect with his son through a poem. For Llewelyn, it was not only the poem that helped him through his homesickness but the fact that his father took the time to write it made all the difference. The strong ties between father and son got Llewelyn through a difficult time in his life. His father was always his anchor.

Spiritual Connections

It is not enough, however, for successful fathers to be simply emotionally linked to their children. They must also be spiritually connected. Strong fathers can bond with their families through family rituals and practices such as family prayer, family scripture study, father-child interviews, and worshipping together. Furthermore, the Holy Ghost can teach men what their children need and when they need it. Lawrence shared the following experience to illustrate this point:

> [My father] may have saved a life by his sensitivity to the Spirit on another occasion. I was hauling a load of beet pulp from west Ogden over the viaduct when Father, who was having a rare moment's leisure to read at home, suddenly closed the book and stood up.
>
> "Where are you going?" Mother called as he hurried down the hall.
>
> "To save Lawrence's life," he called back over his shoulder.
>
> He got into his automobile and met me at the top of the viaduct, just as I was about to start the descent. He reminded me that I was driving a team of four horses abreast (I didn't need a reminder of that!), that they were pulling four tons of beet pulp, and that the wagon had no brakes. While I held the reins, he got out of the car to block a wheel by chaining a spoke to the body of the wagon. Unfortunately, we were holding up traffic, and a car honked behind me. I moved the team to get out of the way, but we had started the descent. The team could not stop. By the time we reached the bottom, the horses were racing out of control on the left side of the road. We hit a car that emerged from behind the candy factory, smashing the motor but sparing the driver. One of the horses slipped and fell down. I seized the momentary check to leap down and sit on his head, keeping him from getting up. We were saved.
>
> If Father had not stopped us and if that car had not come out at that moment, we would have careened onto busy Washington Avenue, Ogden's Main Street, and probably knocked over pedestrians. My feelings of gratitude can only be imagined."[26]

Strong fathers are not only connected with their children, but they are connected to God. They seek for the Spirit in their lives, and that Spirit will lead them to do well. In this example, David may have saved his son's life because he followed the promptings of the Spirit. Similarly, a strong father is also the spiritual leader in his home. He does not shy away from that responsibility; instead, he welcomes the opportunity to bless, serve, and lead his family in righteousness.

From the 1973 pamphlet *Father, Consider Your Ways*, we read:

Fatherhood is leadership, the most important kind of leadership. It has always been so; it always will be so. Father, with the assistance and counsel and encouragement of your eternal companion, you preside in the home. It is not a matter of whether you are most worthy or best qualified, but it is a matter of law and appointment. You preside at the meal table, at family prayer. You preside at family home evening; and as guided by the Spirit of the Lord, you see that your children are taught correct principles. It is your place to give direction relating to all of family life. You give father's blessings. You take an active part in establishing family rules and discipline. As a leader in your home you plan and sacrifice to achieve the blessing of a unified and happy family. To do all of this requires that you live a family-centered life.[27]

David O. McKay was this kind of leader in his home.

The Law of the Harvest

One of the great joys of David's life was watching his children grow in spirituality and become disciples of Jesus Christ. It appeared that all of the hours he and Emma Ray had spent teaching gospel principles in the home, as well as the time they spent working hard at Dry Hollow Farm, paid off. David's children were becoming great contributors to society and the Church. In 1921, David O. McKay had the opportunity to travel Europe as part of the world tour. When President McKay was in France, he was able to connect with Lawrence, who was serving as a missionary in Germany. For ten days, this father-and-son team visited historical sites as well as Church congregations. David invited Lawrence to speak to the Latter-day Saints in their travels. After spending a joyous time with his son, David wrote in his diary, "Seldom, if ever, have I felt a power of joy than that which I experienced in my son's company that evening and succeeding days. The happiness of parenthood, indeed, success in life is dependent upon the honor, intelligence and integrity of our sons and daughters."[28] After David had to part company with Lawrence after ten days of bliss, he wrote, "It was almost as hard to say goodbye to Lawrence at the station as it was a year ago when he left home for his mission. Our most memorable ten days together have served only to make him dearer to me than ever, and I would keep him near to me always."[29] David's connection with his son brought him deep pride, joy, and happiness. Of course, it was also rewarding for him to see firsthand the kind of man Lawrence was becoming.[30] The years of hard work had paid off.

Fathers can build relationships with their children as they invest time and effort. Relationship expert Dr. Wallace H. Goddard explained:

> Children need more than love. They need continuing relationships with the people who love them. People used to talk a lot about quality time with their children. But that seemed to mean, 'I'm going to do something very nice and maybe even spend some money on you. But I only have half an hour, so enjoy it!' That is no way to build a relationship. . . . Relationships include taking time to be with each other. They are also about sensing the other person's unique hopes and wishes. . . . Relationships are not built while running a stopwatch. They grow when people take time to be together. But there is more at issue than time. We need to be in tune with the other person's needs, feelings, and preferences. Sometimes the opportunity to show our love comes at inopportune times and in unexpected ways. . . . For each person there is a different pattern of hopes, dreams, needs, and preferences. The hard part about building relationships is that we must be sensitive to the unique hopes and wishes of the person with whom we would be close.[31]

David O. McKay was a father who discovered ways to create a lasting bond with each of his children. Despite his busy travel schedule, he was able to connect with them on many different levels. Because of this strong bond, he was able to teach and influence them, and he inspired them to be successful professionally, spiritually, and as spouses and parents. It seemed that his children loved him because he first loved them.

Notes

1. David O. McKay, *Gospel Ideals*, 414.

2. Urie Brofenbrenner, "Nobody Home: The Erosion of the American Family," *Psychology Today*, May 1977, 41–47.

3. Madeline Levine, *The Price of Privilege: How Parental Pressure and Material Advantage Are Creating a Generation of Disconnected and Unhappy Kids*, (HarperCollins: New York, 2006), 136.

4. Dollahite, Hawkins, and Brotherson, "Fatherwork: A Conceptual Ethic of Fathering as Generative Work," 32.

5. President Gordon B. Hinckley taught, "Every child is entitled to grow up in a home where there is warm and secure companionship, where there is love in the family relationship, where appreciation one for another is taught and exemplified, and where God is acknowledged and His peace and blessings invoked before the family altar." Gordon B. Hinckley, *Teachings of Gordon B. Hinckley* (Salt Lake City: Deseret Book, 1997), 416.

6. Dollahite, Hawkins, and Brotherson, "Narrative Accounts, Generative Fathering, and Family Life Education," in *The Methods and Methodologies of Qualitative Family Research*, 362.

7. Diaries of David O. McKay, December 1920, MS 668, box 6, folder 1, Marriott Library.

8. Ibid.

9. Diaries of David O. McKay, January to December 1935, MS 668, box 7, folder 13, Marriott Library.

10. Diaries of David O. McKay, May to June 1921, MS 668, box 7, folder 4, Marriott Library.

11. Diaries of David O. McKay, June to July 1921, MS 668, box 7, folder 5, Marriott Library.

12. David O. McKay, in Conference Report, April 1955, 26.

13. David O. McKay, "The True Meaning of Loyalty," *Instructor*, February 1962, 37.

14. Jeanette Morrell, *Highlights in the Life of President David O. McKay* (Salt Lake City: Deseret Book, 1971), 42.

15. L. J. M. Blood, interview by Mary Jane Woodger, 8 August 1995.

16. David L. McKay, interview by Gordon Irving, James Moyle Oral History Program, Salt Lake City, , January–May 1984, 41.

17. McKay, *My Father, David O. McKay*, 73.

18. Llewelyn McKay, *Home Memories of President David O. McKay*, 213.

19. Covey, *Seven Habits of Highly Effective Families*, 152.

20. David O. McKay to Emma Ray McKay, 22 November 1927, David O. McKay Family Papers, 1897–1954, MS 21606, box 1, folder 1, CHL.

21. David O. McKay to Emma Ray McKay, 20 May 1925, David O. McKay Family Papers, 1897–1954, MS 21606, box 1, folder 1, CHL, underline in original.

22. David O. McKay to Emma Ray McKay, 8 December 1910, David O. McKay Family Papers, 1897–1954, MS 21606, box 1, folder 1, CHL.

23. David L. McKay to David O. McKay, 2 May 1914, David O. McKay Papers, MS 668, box 1, folder 3, Marriott Library.

24. Llewelyn R. McKay to David O. McKay, 1 December 1918, David O. McKay Papers, MS 668, box 1, folder 3, Marriott Library.

25. Llewelyn McKay, *Home Memories of President David O. McKay*, 32–33.

26. McKay, *My Father, David O. McKay*, 94.

27. "Father, Consider Your Ways," *Ensign*, June 2002, 12–15.

28. Diaries of David O. McKay, October–December 1921, MS 668, box 6, folder 10, Marriott Library.

29. Ibid.

30. Of course, David was not only proud of Lawrence, he was extremely pleased with all of his children. Each one of them proved to be successful individuals. At the age of sixty-three, he wrote in his diary that Lou Jean and Russell were in medical school in Cleveland, Ohio; David L. had graduated from Harvard Law School and practiced law in Salt Lake City, Llewelyn finished his PhD at Stanford and was teaching at the University of Utah, Emma Rae taught at Granite High School, Edward was a missionary, and Robert was president of the senior class at his high school. See Diaries of David O. McKay, January to December 1937, MS 668, box 8, folder 2, Marriott Library. One can almost visualize President McKay's buttons bursting for the pride he had for his children. He raised a wonderful posterity.

31. Goddard, *The Frightful and Joyous Journey of Family Life*, 96–97.

8

Going with the Flow

"God has implanted deep in the souls of parents the truth that they cannot with impunity shirk the responsibility to protect childhood and youth."
—David O. McKay[1]

One of the great characteristics of teachers and leaders of youth is flexibility. Adults who have been given the charge to work with children and teens should understand the need to adapt and change according to the situation. After all, teens are often changing their minds as well as their direction. Good leaders and teachers can adapt to the circumstance. Fathers who also can adapt and be flexible will be successful.

Children change, grow, and mature throughout their lifespan. For each stage of their lives, their needs change. Successful fathers are able to change and acclimate to their children at various times and in different circumstances. Change and flexibility "can mean making shifts in one's job or lifestyle for more time and energy with children."[2] If a father has multiple children, those personalities will be unique in their own way, and diverse personality styles will be the cause of a diversity of interactions, challenges, and opportunities. For example, an oldest child's passions, dreams, and interests may be very different than a younger child's. Therefore, fathers must adapt from child to child and change their

David O. and Emma McKay as grandparents. (Courtesy of Intellectual Reserve, Inc.)

parenting styles to best fit particular situations. Obviously, a father cannot expect the same from his eighteen-year-old son as he would from a preschool-aged daughter.

Flexibility also implies being able to "go with the flow" and to keep your wits when there is a crisis. A father with this trait also does not get locked into thinking that his way is the only way to accomplish a certain task or that his idea is the only correct way to do something.

David O. McKay seemed able to adapt to most parenting situations, regardless of the stage of life or the circumstance. At one point in his life, he had to minister to his younger children, his children who were married, and his grandchildren. He appeared to do a excellent job meeting the needs of his children at every stage of their lives, regardless of their age.

Going with the Flow

Lawrence shared the experience of traveling with his father and mother to California when he was eight years old. When young Lawrence saw the ocean for the first time, his curiosity was piqued, and he deeply desired to pay a visit to the seashore. After a good night's rest, Lawrence decided to explore the beach. He related the following:

> I woke up very early next morning and set off with innocent enthusiasm to inspect the ocean close up, an expedition that involved crossing the speedway. The ocean was much more exciting this time. The tide was coming in, and the waves were thundering on the beach. I was totally engrossed in the spectacle when I realized, after

some time, that someone was beside me. It was Father. He smiled at me and said, 'It's beautiful, isn't it?' Then, hand in hand, we went back and had breakfast.

In retrospect, particularly as a father myself, I can imagine how alarmed Mother and Father were when they awoke to find me gone and with what concern Father set out to look for me. But finding me safe, he chose not to communicate any part of that alarm to me. Instead, he simply shared the beauty of the ocean with me and made it an unforgettable memory for me.[3]

Part of David O. McKay's wisdom and flexibility was his ability to always value relationships over rules or expectations. In the case of the "morning explorer," it would have been easy for him to chastise his son or rebuke him for his wandering. Instead, David used this opportunity to connect with Lawrence and have a bonding moment together—something that was probably rare in the life of this busy Apostle. Preserving the relationship he had with his children was always paramount, more so than rules and regulations.

Animal Farm

Another change in David's parenting is evidenced by the experiences that occurred as he tried to teach his children responsibility. He strongly believed that one of the best ways to instill responsibility was by having his children take care of animals. Lawrence was responsible for the family cow, and Llewelyn raised the chickens. There was also a family boar named Caesar. On one occasion when David was trying to hurry out the door to catch a train, he noticed that Caesar had broken out of his pen and was trotting down the street. Because time was of the essence, David had to hurry quickly to catch the boar, put him in the chicken coop, and make a mad dash for the train station. At 2:00 a.m. the phone rang at the McKay home, and the operator announced that there was a telegram for Mr. Lawrence McKay. "With their father away and such an unexpected call at such an obscure hour, the family feared the worse. Lawrence scribbled down the urgent message as the operator read him the telegram: 'Caesar in chicken coop! Water him!' Lawrence thanked the operator, and the entire house laughed with relief. One of the boys exclaimed, 'That's all the telegram said? Father must really love that ugly boar!'"[4]

One spring, Lawrence had untied the family cow so she could drink. She got away, and Lawrence was not sure where to find her. He approached his father to report that he had lost the cow. How would his father respond? Would David O. McKay be upset? Would he be angry? Would he convey disappointment? The answer is none of the above. Instead, David said to his son, "She's probably started on her way to Huntsville. Let's go and see." As they traveled up the canyon, they discovered that someone had found the cow and tied her to a telephone pole partway up the canyon. "Father took the rope, wound it around her neck, and put a note on her halter: 'Please let me pass, I'm going to grass.'"[5] Both father and son had a great laugh. Instead of rebuking his son or giving him a lesson on obedience and responsibility, David O. McKay seized the opportunity to spend some one-on-one time with his son and have a great laugh together.

Seasoned Fathering

President and Sister McKay still had young children at home when they were in their early sixties. In 1935, Lawrence would have been thirty-four; Llewelyn was thirty-one; and Lou Jean was twenty-nine. However, their younger children were still in high school and college. Emma Rae was twenty-two; Edward was twenty; and Bobby was fifteen. Like most men, President McKay had less energy and less stamina as he aged, especially when compared to his earlier years as a parent. Instead of working a full day at the Church Office Building in Salt Lake City and then heading to Huntsville to haul hay in the evening, David's pace slowed with age. He still worked harder than the average man his age, and Ned and Bobby were constantly taken to Huntsville for work projects. However, President McKay expanded his involvement with his children into other areas. For example, he began to take more interest in taking his children to movies. His diaries are full of accounts of visiting picture shows, meeting his children at the theater, and taking the family to Fish Lake for some needed recreation.[6] In fact, although President McKay did not vacation that often with his older children, the younger children (Emma Rae, Ned, and Bobby) were the beneficiaries of visits to Yellowstone National Park and other exciting places.[7] And when it was time for Ned to leave for the German-Austria Mission, President McKay spent the day before his departure purchasing suitcases, clothing, and anything else a departing missionary might need.[8]

These are the type of fatherly activities that David may not have engaged in during his younger years. However, as he aged, he adapted to the needs of his children and took any opportunity he could to spend time with them. In a way, he changed his parenting philosophy from taking his sons to the family farm to doing things with his children that they seemed to enjoy.

Because David knew that the time he had with his children was precious, he seized those opportunities. Instead of focusing on correction or discipline, David was centered on building relationships. He understood from his professional teaching experience that the only way to influence young people is to have a connection with them. He also understood that to impact young people, parents and teachers must adapt and speak the youth's language.

For example, as an Apostle in the Church, there is no question that David O. McKay was doctrinally sound. He could dialogue with the greatest scholars as a theologian and as an educator. However, he adjusted his approach when he taught children. He would use visual aids and object lessons to capture their attention. When a mother asked her children what they enjoyed most about a chapel dedication in California, one of them responded, "President McKay spoke to us children, and we could understand what he meant."[9] Being able to adapt, change, and be flexible are traits of a strong and healthy father.

David O. McKay demonstrated this strength on many levels throughout his life. He understood that there is a time and season for everything. Most often, he valued relationships over rules. As a result, he formed a strong bond with each of his children. President McKay understood the importance of being flexible, and he seemed to improve with time as he learned to meet the needs of each child and grandchild.

Notes

1.   David O. McKay, in Conference Report, April 1969, 7.

2.   Dollahite, Hawkins, and Brotherson, "Fatherwork: A Conceptual Ethic of Fathering as Generative Work," 32.

3.   McKay, *My Father, David O. McKay*, 100–101; see also David L. McKay, address at a Luncheon of the 17th Annual Meeting of the Mormon History Association, 8 May 1982, microfilm, MS 7013, CHL.

4.   Gary W. Toyn and Michael K. Winder, *Life Lessons from Fathers of Faith: Inspiring True Stories about Latter-day Dads* (American Fork, UT: Covenant Communications, 2010), 47.

5.   David L. McKay, interview by Gordon Irving, James Moyle Oral History Program, Salt Lake City, January–May 1984, 12.

6.   Diaries of David O. McKay, January–December 1935, MS 668, box 7, folder 13, Marriott Library.

7.   Diaries of David O. McKay, January–December 1937, MS 668, box 8, folder 2, Marriott Library.

8.   Diaries of David O. McKay, January–October 1936, MS 668, box 7, folder 14, Marriott Library.

9.   Gregory A. Prince and Wm. Robert Wright, *David O. McKay and the Rise of Modern Mormonism* (Salt Lake City: University of Utah Press, 2005), 17.

Epilogue

President David O. McKay was not a perfect father or husband; however, he was driven by the desire to be a disciple of Jesus Christ. He taught that "members of the Church are under obligation to make the sinless son of man their ideal. He is the one perfect being who ever walked the earth; the sublimest example of nobility; godlike in nature, perfect in his love; our Redeemer; our Savior; the immaculate Son of our Eternal Father; the Light, the Life, the Way."[1] It was President McKay's mission to become as much like our Savior, Jesus Christ, as he possibly could. He sought to develop the Christlike attributes of patience, mercy, kindness, and charity. Above anyone else, members of his family were the beneficiaries of his quest toward a Christlike life.

Besides striving to live as the Savior, President McKay also found ways to connect himself to his children. He lived in an era where men were just beginning to take a more active role in parenting and discipline. Arguably, he was busier than most of his contemporaries, yet he found ways to be involved with his children in every aspect of their lives—from sports, to music, to academics, to spirituality. Because of his positive relationship with his children, they accepted his beliefs and ideals, and they desired to be with him as often as they could—even if that meant spending a day laboring on their farm or traveling abroad with him on Church assignments. Speaking of his parents, Lawrence explained, "We learned to love them because they first dearly loved each other and us."[2]

Furthermore, President McKay never wanted his children to feel obligated to "live right" or "be good" because of the high position he held in the Church. Instead, he seemed to desire more than anything else that his children would do the right things for the right reasons. He wanted them to do good because that is how disciples of Jesus Christ should behave. He taught his children, as well as the membership of the Church, that "the highest of all ideals are the teachings and particularly the life of Jesus of Nazareth, and that man is most truly great who is most Christlike. What you sincerely in your heart think of Christ will determine what you are, will largely determine what your acts will be."[3] President McKay pointed his children toward the Savior by what he taught and certainly by how he lived.

President David O. McKay made his family his highest priority. Even though he was pulled in many directions by his employment, church service, civic duties, and even farm responsibilities, he made sure that his family came first. Contemporary fathers should be able to relate to President McKay in terms of his busy schedule and his efforts to balance work, family, and Church responsibilities. President McKay identified what was most important in his life, and then he acted accordingly. His teachings about the family were not mere rhetoric or lip service. He truly lived as he taught. In a general conference, he declared:

> One of our most precious possessions is our families. The domestic relations precede, and, in our present existence, are worth more than all other social ties. They give the first throb to the heart and unseal the deep fountains of its love. Home is the chief school of human virtues. Its responsibilities, joys, sorrows, smiles, tears, hopes, and solicitudes form the chief interests of human life. . . .

When one puts business or pleasure above his home, he that moment starts on the downgrade to soul-weakness. When the club becomes more attractive to any man than his home, it is time for him to confess in bitter shame that he has failed to measure up to the supreme opportunity of his life and flunked in the final test of true manhood. . . . The poorest shack in which love prevails over a united family is of greater value to God and future humanity than any other riches. In such a home God can work miracles and will work miracles.[4]

President McKay's beliefs and perceptions about parenthood are timeless. His example and teachings can benefit all families and fathers today. The challenges that David O. McKay faced as a father years ago are not very different than the struggles that accompany contemporary fatherhood. Modern fathers should look to President David O. McKay as a role model of successful fatherhood and follow his example of how to navigate through the difficult, yet joyous times of parenthood.

Notes

1. David O. McKay, *Treasures of Life*, ed. Clare Middlemiss (Whitefish, MT: Literary Licensing, 2011), 210.

2. McKay, *My Father, David O. McKay*, 99.

3. David O. McKay, in Conference Report, April 1951, 93.

4. David O. McKay, in Conference Report, April 1964, 5.

About the Author

Mark D. Ogletree is an associate professor in the Department of Church History and Doctrine. Mark taught for twenty-one years in the Church Educational System, where he was a seminary teacher, seminary principal, institute instructor, institute director, and Church Educational System coordinator. He received his bachelor's degree in human resource development from Brigham Young University; his master's degree in mental health counseling and educational psychology from Northern Arizona University, and his PhD in family and human development from Utah State University. Before coming to BYU, Mark owned and operated his own marriage and family therapy practice in McKinney, Texas. He has written several books on marriage and family–related topics. Mark and his wife, Janie, have eight children and nine grandchildren and reside in Provo, Utah.

Index